TEACHING WITH THE

BEST of
Instructor

NEW YORK • TORONTO • LONDON • AUCKLAND • SYDNEY
MEXICO CITY • NEW DELHI • HONG KONG • BUENOS AIRES

Answers to Reproducible Activities

Multiplication Mysteries, pages 25–7.

Mystery Trick or Treat Bag, page 25.

1. $5 \times 6 = 30$
2. $7 \times 2 = 14$
3. $4 \times 2 = 8$
4. $3 \times 8 = 24$
5. $6 \times 3 = 18$
6. $3 \times 11 = 33$

Bat Wing Stew Reproducible, page 26.

$6 \times 3 =$ 18 monster eyes
$1 \times 1 =$ 1 rattlesnake rattle
$4 \times 8 =$ 32 lizard legs
$8 \times 9 =$ 72 spider legs
$2 \times 7 =$ 14 bat wings
$10 \times 1/2 =$ 5 cups of pond water

Mystery Mansion Reproducible, page 27.

Bats: $6 \times 2 = 12$
Ghosts: $3 \times 6 = 18$
Jack-o'-lanterns: $4 \times 6 = 24$
Spiders: $3 \times 8 = 24$
Black cats: $5 \times 4 = 20$
Monsters: $4 \times 3 = 12$
Trick-or-treaters: $2 \times 2 = 4$

Bats Challenge Reproducible, page 30.

Flying Fox Bat: This giant, fluffy bat has a face that makes it look like a fox.

Bumblebee Bat: This tiny bat is the smallest kind of bat in the world.

Vampire Bat: This bat uses its fangs to feed on cows, pigs, and mules.

Bulldog (Fisherman) Bat: This bat swoops out of the sky and catches fish for its dinner.

Little Brown Bat: This plain brown bat is the most common bat in the United States.

Big-Eared Bat: This bat looks like a rabbit with its big ears and nose.

Meet the Explorers Reproducible, page 34.

1. Eriksson
2. Columbus
3. Magellan
4. De Leon
5. Cabot
6. Drake

Dr. Seuss Crossword Puzzle Reproducible, page 69.

Across	Down
1. Hop	**1.** Hooray
4. Oobleck	**2.** Wocket
5. Moo	**3.** Foot
6. Zebra	**7.** Butter
8. Yertle	**9.** Eyes
10. Hats	**11.** Places
12. Blue	**13.** Hears
14. Grinch	**17.** Circus
15. Ran	
16. Socks	
18. Green	

Equator Map Hunt Reproducible, page 79.

1. Quito, Ecuador
2. Kampala, Uganda
3. Singapore, Singapore
4. Libreville, Gabon
5. Nairobi, Kenya
ANSWER: Raincoat

■ ■ ■

Page 75: From THE FOUR SEASONS: JAPANESE HAIKU written by Basho, Buson, Issa, Shiki, and many others; translated by Peter Beilenson. Reprinted by permission of Peter Pauper Press.

Cover illustration by Patrick Girouard, cover design by Dan Schultz, interior design by Johari Fuentes and Norma Ortiz.
Interior illustrations: pages 12–14 by Kevin Henkes and Patrick Girouard, page 16 by Cary Pillo, pages 54–58 by Eduardo Rosado, pages 74–76 by Christy Hale, pages 93–94 by Mike Moran. All other illustrations by Patrick Girouard.

ISBN 0-439-74322-2

Contents

Back to School

Standards-Based Activities

Following Directions, Working With Others, Active Listening,
Cooperation, Solving Problems, Learning Vocabulary, and More!

We are on our way!

Back to ARTS & CRAFTS

Bus Buddies

Students will get a chance to meet and greet their new classmates as they fill in the bus windows with pictures of their new buddies.

For this project, you'll need three 1-1/4" wood circles, yellow and black construction paper if desired, craft items (such as yarn and googly eyes), and the bus **Reproducible**, page 8.

1. Color and cut out the school bus, or trace it onto yellow construction paper and add your own colorful details, such as your school's name.

2. Cut out the bus wheels and glue them onto the bus as shown.

3. Use the wood circles to make faces for the bus windows. Decorate them with yarn hair and googly eyes. Use markers for smiles.

4. Glue each "buddy" onto a bus window. Draw additional details as desired.

Tip: Wood circles can be purchased at a craft store. As an alternative, have children color white soda bottle lids with crayons to make their bus buddies.
—*Adapted from an idea by Linda Zajac, Vernon, CT*

Wiggly Worm Nametag

Wear these interactive nametags or use them in a get-to-know-you game of "Guess Who?"

For each wiggly worm nametag, you'll need markers or crayons, scissors, tape or glue, and the apple and worm **Reproducible** on page 9.

1. Color and cut out the apple and worm patterns.

2. Cut out and glue or tape a leaf to the apple.

3. Write your name on the worm. Accordion-fold the worm, leaving about 1" at the head end.

4. Glue or tape the worm to the inside of the circle opening, as shown. To display your name, stretch the worm out to full length. Re-fold and tuck the worm into the hole to hide your name.

Tip: After the class is finished wearing the nametags, use them in a center. Ask children to write a "Guess Who?" clue on the apple such as "I have red hair." Unfold the worm for the answer!

JOHARI

Personal Pyramid

Invite students to share several sides of their personalities with these unique picture frames.

For each pyramid, you'll need a small photo of each child, yarn, markers or crayons, glue, and the pyramid **Reproducible** on page 9.

❶ Cut out the pyramid Reproducible.

❷ Cut and glue the photo to fit inside the small triangle, as shown.

❸ On each of the remaining sides, invite students to draw something that represents them, such as a favorite pet or hobby.

❹ Fold the pyramid along the dotted lines. Then glue the tabs in place, as shown, to create a pyramid. Trap the ends of a piece of yarn in the top of the pyramid to make a loop hanger.

Tip: Instead of drawing, children might want to try collage—glueing small photos or pictures from magazines onto their pyramids.

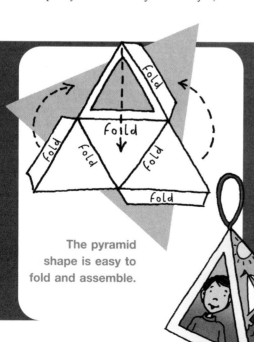

The pyramid shape is easy to fold and assemble.

fold fold fold fold fold fold

School

School's in! Set students' minds and fingers in motion with wonderful welcome-back crafts
By Mackie Rhodes

Study Zone Door Hanger

When it's time for homework, these personalized signs help students send a loud and clear message—without making a sound!

For each sign, you'll need four wide craft sticks, 5-1/2" black construction paper square, 10" length of yarn, chalk, and small "school supply" stickers.

❶ To create a mini-chalkboard, glue the craft sticks around the black square, trapping each end of the yarn in a glued corner to make a hanger. Allow the glue to dry.

❷ Use chalk to write "[Name]'s Study Zone" on the chalkboard.

❸ Decorate open spaces on the chalkboard with stickers. To display, hang your mini-chalkboard on a doorknob.

Tip: To keep the chalk from smearing, coat it lightly with clear acrylic craft spray or hair spray.

—Lucia Henry, Fallon, NV

Sculpt a Neighborhood

Start the year by making a mural of your community. Children can "sculpt" houses, a school, a fire station, stores, and other important buildings, creating a fascinating textured display.

For this art center, you'll need newspaper, construction paper in many different colors, poster paint, scissors, and glue. After acquainting your students with the many types of buildings in your community, guide them through the following steps:

1. Cut construction paper into the building shape of your choice.

twist paper

2. Tear the newspaper into strips, then twist or crumple them. Glue the strips onto your building, shaping and sculpting them to form features such as windows, doors, and a roof. If desired, use paint to add more details and texture.

Tip: To avoid getting newsprint on their clothes, have children wear paint smocks as they work.

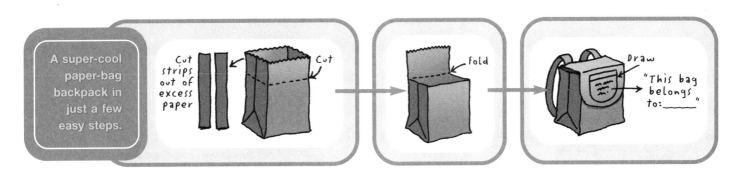

A super-cool paper-bag backpack in just a few easy steps.

Paper-Bag Backpacks

Make these bags during your first week back and use them as "getting to know you" icebreakers. Children can fill them with photographs, drawings of favorite things, and small treasures to share.

For each backpack, you'll need a paper lunch bag, markers or crayons, and scissors.

❶ Open the bag. Cut off the front and sides of the bag about 5" from the top, as shown. Cut out two 1" wide straps from the removed section of the bag.

❷ Fold the tall side of the bag over the front to create a flap. Trim the flap in a semi-circular shape.

❸ Glue the straps to the back.

❹ Decorate the bag to resemble a school backpack.

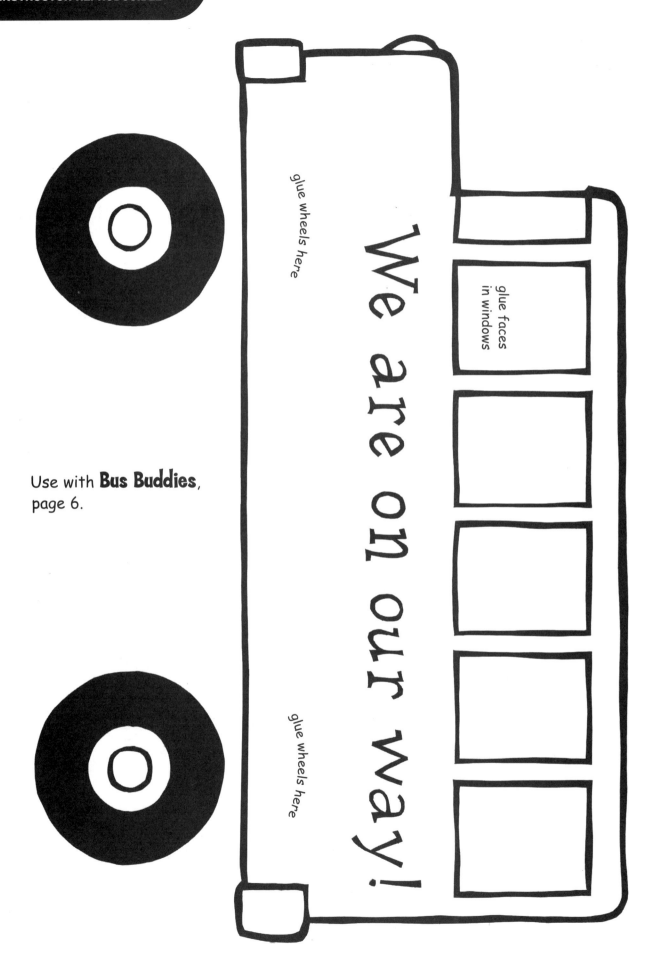

glue wheels here

glue faces in windows

We are on our way!

Use with **Bus Buddies**, page 6.

glue wheels here

Use with **Personal Pyramid**, page 6.

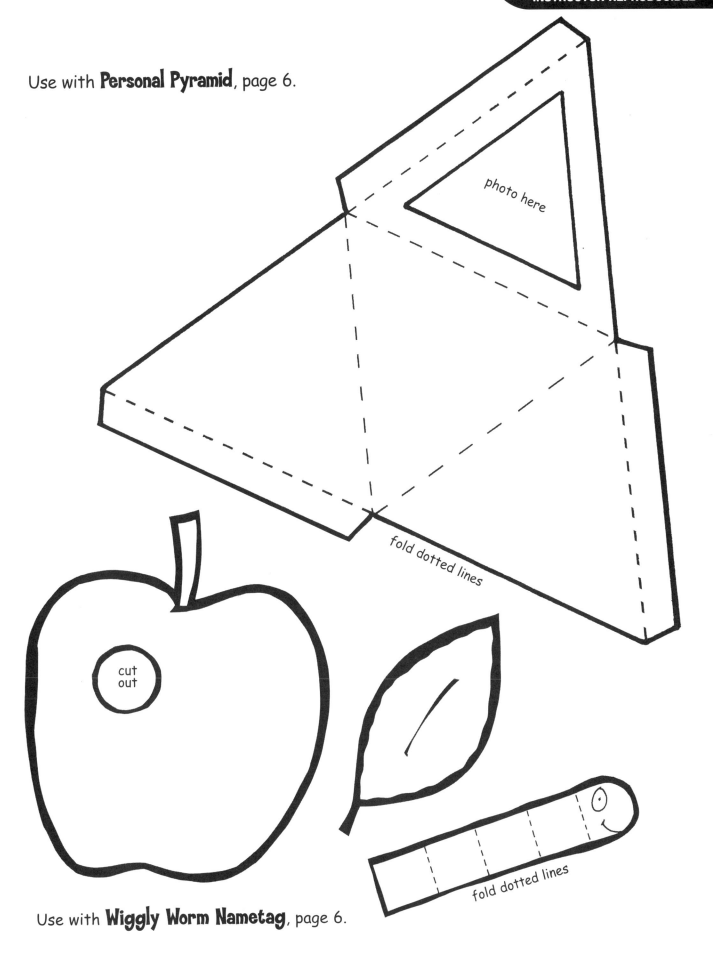

photo here

fold dotted lines

cut out

Use with **Wiggly Worm Nametag**, page 6.

fold dotted lines

THE FIRST DAY

Build community spirit with opening day activities from teachers like you

I'm Puzzled

Learning names helps children feel recognized and build connections with one another. Here's a great hands-on way to help students learn to read and spell their new classmates' names. Print each child's name on a sentence strip, leaving space between each letter. Cut between the letters of each name to make a letter-scramble puzzle. Place each puzzle in an envelope labeled with the child's name and randomly distribute the envelopes to student workspaces. Invite children to move from puzzle to puzzle, putting the letters of their classmates' names in order. Encourage them to use the name on the envelope to check their work.
—*Sharon Coleridge, Wicoff School, Plainsboro, NJ*

"All About Me" Pictures

Ask your new students if they've ever heard the expression "A picture is worth a thousand words." Discuss what it means and then tell students that instead of using words to tell about themselves, they will be creating posters to let pictures do the talking. Give each child a sheet of poster board, and set up worktables with lots of art supplies as well as magazines to cut. Invite children to fill their poster board with pictures that say something about themselves—for example, images that represent favorite foods, sports they enjoy, pets they have, places they like, and so on. Let children take turns sharing their posters, letting classmates look at the pictures and make guesses about their interests.
—*Natalie Vaughn, Phoenix School, Encinitas, CA*

We're a Perfect Fit!

Create this bulletin board on the first day to demonstrate how each student plays an important part in building a classroom community. Cut out puzzle pieces from a sheet of poster board to equal the number of students in your class. On a second sheet of poster board, create an outline of the puzzle to show how the pieces fit together. Staple the outline to the bulletin board along with the words "Room _____ is a perfect fit!" On the first day of school, give each student a puzzle piece to decorate with their name, picture, and words or objects that describe them. Work together with students to reconstruct the puzzle by taping the pieces to the outline on the bulletin board. Gather children around the completed puzzle. Explain that this puzzle represents your classroom community—each child is an individual, yet everyone must work together to create a safe and caring classroom.
—*Cindy Chinn and Marianne Chang, Schilling School, Newark, CA*

Three Little-Known Facts

Challenge your students to write three little-known facts about themselves. Older students who have shared classes before will need to think hard to come up with facts that their classmates don't already know. Begin by sharing three facts about yourself—for example, "I am a marathon runner,"

"One summer I swam in three seas," and "I love dried cranberries." Collect the little-known facts, read them aloud, and guess who belongs to each set of facts. The children love this assignment because it satisfies their curiosity about one another's unique talents, experiences, and passions.
—*Marcee Chapman, Mountain View, CA*

First-Day Drama

Play charades to learn about your students' interests! Ask each student to write down a few of their favorite hobbies or interests and pass the papers to you. Group children together who share similar interests. Let each group first figure out what they have in common. Then they can work together to figure out how to act out their hobby or interest using only actions and gestures. Encourage students to use complete sentences and classmates' names (for instance, "Jordan and Jonathon like to play the guitar") when they make their guesses.
—*Barbara Sheridan, Dutch Neck School, Princeton Junction, NJ*

Left and Right Pencil Pass

Build classroom community with this fun round-robin game that challenges students to listen carefully and think quickly. Write a quick story that includes many "left" and "right" words. For example: *I left home this morning thinking I would go right to school. Then I realized I left my lunch right on the kitchen table. I turned right around and went back home.* Give each child a new, unsharpened pencil. Each time you say "left" or "right," students should pass their pencils to the next person in that direction. Speed up the game as you go, making it more and more challenging for students to keep up. At the end of the game, make sure each student has a new pencil to keep as his or her own.
—*Pamela Galus, Omaha Public Schools, Omaha, NE*

Toss and Tell

This icebreaker combines math and reading to spark a lively round of sharing among students. Make two oversized number cubes by covering square tissue boxes with craft paper. On one cube, write the numbers 1 to 6. On the other, write things that children can tell about themselves, for example: "my favorite stories," "things I like to do," "places I've visited," "my favorite foods," and "words that describe me." Gather children in a circle and model the game by going first. Toss the cubes, then tell something about yourself based on how they land—for example, if you rolled a 3 and "my favorite foods," you would then name three foods that you like. Let the children continue, taking turns tossing the cubes and telling about themselves.
—*Deborah Rovin-Murphy, Richboro Elementary School, Richboro, PA*

Push My Button

Help students become "user-friendly" by "installing" buttons that classmates can push to reveal information to one another. Give each student a large button to wear that reads "Press This Button." On an index card, have them respond to questions such as:
- What is your name?
- When is your birthday?
- What is your favorite subject?

The children will enjoy helping you create the questions. Then invite students to mill around the room for a set period of time. When a classmate "pushes their button," they should respond like a robot and read the information written on their card. Challenge each student to ask questions of 10 classmates! Make sure to make a button for yourself so students can learn about you, too.
—*Judy Wetzel, Woodburn School, Falls Church, VA*

Flashcard Match-ups

Have kids brush up on last year's math skills as they meet and greet one another with this fun-filled flashcard game. Distribute math fact cards to half your students and corresponding answer cards to the other half. When you say "go," each child should quickly find his or her math fact partner and then sit down. When all the children have found their matches, have them take turns sharing their math facts and the answers. Then challenge students to play an even faster second round of the game!
—*Michele Stevens, Charleston Public Schools, Charleston, WV*

Make Your Class a Community With
Kevin Henkes

By Mackie Rhodes

Will I have friends in class? Will I enjoy my new classroom? Will I fit in? Everyone is nervous the first day back. Help ease those September anxieties with these cross-curricular, community-building activities based on popular Kevin Henkes books.

Before You Begin

Decide how much time you plan to spend on your author study: one book per week, or a concentrated first-week unit. Gather and read all the wonderful Kevin Henkes books and become familiar with the characters' personalities, relationships, and conflicts. Set up your reading center with multiple copies of all the titles for individual and group reading. You may want to ask volunteers to record a selection of Kevin Henkes books on tape for a listening center. A bulletin board with book jackets, an author photo, and a place to display the upcoming student work is a great "advertisement" for the unit to help get your class started.

A Worrying Scroll

In *Wemberly Worried*, little mouse Wemberly worries with the best of them! Review her list of concerns about the first day of school. Is she worried about whether or not she will fit in? As a class, make worry scrolls that list all your worries about the upcoming year. Beside each worry, have students write what, if anything, helps to ease their worries—a new friend, being reacquainted with old friends, a fun teacher, or a favorite activity. Have them roll up their lists and tie them with yarn. Later, invite students to share their scrolls with a partner and compare their worries and solutions.

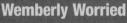

When We Belong, We Bloom!

What makes your students feel that they fit into your class? Common interests, working together, making friends, and feeling accepted are a few things that help kids feel a sense of belonging or community. Invite children to cut out and label large paper flower petals with ways in which they each fit into their class community. They might write, "We pay attention," "We tell great stories," or "We always play fair." Assemble the petals into a large flower, write "Our Class" in the center and then display it with the heading "When We Belong, We Bloom!"

Make a Friendship Chain

In *Chester's Way*, two friends become three. In your class, three friends can become four, four friends five, and so on. To demonstrate how a community of

Wemberly Worried

Wemberly's first-day-of-school worries begin to fade when she meets Jewel. Before school ends, the two girls discover that they've had a fun and almost worry-free day.

"Wemberly worried about everything. Big things, little things, and things in-between."

friendship can grow, have your class create a Friendship Chain. To begin, make a simple "friend" pattern, like the one illustrated below, and give one to each student.

Ask the children to color in their "friends" and cut them out. Then, working together, students attach all the friends by taping or glueing the hands together. The class will enjoy working together on this project and watching the chain grow and grow.

Everyone's a Teacher

Lilly taught Chester and Wilson lots of new things—like talking backwards and

cutting sandwiches with cookie cutters. Everyone has something to teach. Invite children, one at a time, to take the role of teacher. Ask each child to teach something he or she knows to a small group, or to the whole class. Students might teach the class how to say a few words in a foreign language, how to play a game, or how to fix a bike. They might show their classmates how to draw stars, make up jokes, or care for a guinea pig. With every "lesson," children will develop an appreciation for their own and their classmates' talents as well as gain a greater sense of community.

The Lightbulb Lab

In *Lilly's Purple Plastic Purse*, when Lilly and her classmates are in the mood to think of great ideas, they go to the Lightbulb Lab and express themselves through drawing and writing. Set up a lightbulb lab for your students. Ask the children to draw and cut out paper lightbulbs. On their lightbulbs, they can write great ideas for making the classroom successful. Use the lightbulbs to decorate the lab and fill a bookshelf with exciting reference materials for sparking creative thinking.

Weigh the Consequences

Was Lilly's excitement over her purse a benefit or a burden to her class? Invite children to find out by weighing the consequences. Label one side of a scale

benefit and the other side *burden*. Then place a clear plastic tumbler on each side. Review the story with your class and look closely at each instance in which Lilly brought out her purse. Did the class gain something positive from the purse? Or did the purse create a problem for the class? Have the children put a counter into the appro-

priate cup for each: *benefit* or *burden*. Before adding each counter, encourage them to predict what will happen to the scale. In which direction will it tip by the end of the activity? Was the purse a benefit or burden?

A Community Journal

Start the new school year with a cooperative journal your students share as the class develops into a community. Encourage the children to write about class events and experiences by letting them take turns bringing the journal home and adding to it. To help reinforce the concept of community, occasionally have the whole class write

Chrysanthemum • When classmates tease her, Chrysanthemum begins to dislike her once absolutely perfect name. That is, until her well-loved music teacher shares her opinion of Chrysanthemum's name and the class instantly changes its tune!

"'Hooray!' said Chrysanthemum. 'School!' But when Mrs. Chud took roll call, everyone giggled upon hearing Chrysanthemum's name."

about a special event and add these pages into the classroom journal. Later in the year, you can use the journal to reminisce and review.

Meet the Teacher

In *Lilly's Purple Plastic Purse*, Mr. Slinger tells his students, in both actions and words, to be yourself and you will fit in. Follow Mr. Slinger's example to help children develop an appreciation for the unique individuals in their class and see how they fit perfectly into the class community. To begin, share a sampling of unique things about yourself, such as a collection, pictures of a pet, or your favorite music. Then display photos and stories about yourself on a bulletin board. Invite students to write and illustrate their impressions of you

to add to your teacher display. To strengthen appreciation of everyone's individuality, change the board to "Meet the Student," and celebrate a student each week.

First Day Story Strips

Chrysanthemum had many ups and downs on her first day of school. After reading the story, ask children to create folding story strips that sequence their own experiences of the first day of school. What do they remember about their first classroom, their first friend? Share the story strips with class read-alouds.

Closing Activity— Make Your Own Mouse

End your Kevin Henkes unit with a mouse show! Invite your students to invent their own mouse characters. Begin by encouraging them to create significant details by asking specific questions: "What kind of shoes does your mouse character like?" or "What hobbies does your mouse have?" When the children have their list of details, ask them to write character descriptions and work together in groups to write a story or short play. Celebrate all your great work with a class read-aloud day! ■

KEVIN HENKES READING CORNER

- Wemberley Worried, 2000.
- Lilly's Purple Plastic Purse, 1996.
- The Biggest Boy, 1995.
- Owen, 1993.
- A Weekend with Wendell, 1992.
- Chrysanthemum, 1991.
- Julius, the Baby of the World, 1990.
- Jessica, 1989.
- Chester's Way, 1988.

All books published by Greenwillow.

Lilly's Purple Plastic Purse

When Lilly's favorite teacher, Mr. Slinger, puts Lilly's favorite musical purse away for the day, she experiences a range of emotions.

Chester's Way

Best friends Chester and Wilson do everything the same way, just like two peas in a pod. Then along comes Lilly, who has her own ways of doing things!

"LiLLY loved school. She loved the pointy pencils. She loved the squeaky chalk. And she loved the way her boots went clickety-clickety-clack down the long shiny hallways."

WELCOMING SECOND-LANGUAGE LEARNERS

By Kama Einhorn

Terrific techniques to ease students into the school year

Classroom Buddies

Assign your newcomer child a classroom buddy, preferably bilingual, to conduct a school tour and to help with classroom introductions and routines. Rotate buddies through the first week and month, if possible, so that different children get a chance.

A Family Welcome

Plan an initial parent conference to find out as much as you can about the student and his or her home culture. Have parents bring a translator or provide one. Ask: "What has your child's previous schooling experience been like?" "What does your child like to read?" "What are your hopes for your child this year?"

Language Reminders

Build a foundation for communication by giving your newcomer a recent picture of the class marked with the names of all students. Then share the **Reproducible**, page 16; have the newcomer write each word in his or her native language below the pictures. Hand out copies of the completed page so that all students can have a bilingual reference sheet, flashcards, or concentration game cards.

Stress-Free Environment

Keep stress levels low—and performance high—with appropriate language demands. Another way to lower anxiety is to correct mistakes indirectly. For example, if a child says, "Yesterday I make a cake," you can say, "Yesterday you made a cake? Great!" Also, when placing the child in a cooperative group, give him or her a specific role that isn't too dependent on language skills.

Sheltering Strategies

Sheltering is the use of strategies for providing newcomer children with language they can understand. Here are some teaching techniques to try:

- *Pre-teach all important vocabulary words.*
- *Speak slowly, using short, simple sentences.*
- *Write out directions and suggestions on the board; seeing words aids literacy.*
- *Use hand and facial gestures as you speak. These aid comprehension.*
- *Use visual cues such as pictures, maps, and diagrams. These help all learners.*
- *If possible, have a volunteer review lessons in the child's native language.*
- *When you can, keep read-alouds and instructions to the class short, and read these more than once.*

• Whose turn is it?
• I understand
• Can you speak more slowly, please?

Assessing Language Skills

Choose a private place, and a time when the student seems relaxed. For speaking assessment, show the child a picture of an action. Ask, "What is happening here?" As the child speaks, notice the vocabulary, pronunciation, grammar patterns, and so on. For listening, ask questions such as "What is your name?" "Where are you from?" and "How old are you?" Next, sit with a box of crayons and small objects such as pennies, jellybeans, jacks, etc. Give simple commands such as "Give me the red crayon" or "Show me three." For reading, choose text just below grade level. See if he or she can read aloud and ask simple comprehension questions. If not, go down one more level. For writing, ask the child to write about his or her home, family, or friends. If he or she cannot write anything, invite him or her to draw a picture.

Use with **Language Reminders**, page 15.

Cut along the dotted lines.

student	teacher	scissors	crayons	clock

book	notebook	friends	map	calendar

desk	chair	paper	pencil	glue

Fall

Standards-Based Activities

Reading for Meaning, Critical Thinking, Reading Charts & Graphs,
Practicing Math Facts, Using Maps, and Much More

FALL Activities
From Our Readers

Mathball Game

As a second-grade teacher, I often see students getting frustrated and giving up on math. For a welcome change from math drills at their desks, I invite my class to play a game of Mathball. This activity has led to an increase in students' willingness to learn math—and in their basic computational skills—since they learn best when they are doing an activity that is fun. Before beginning, acquire two small inflatable or sponge balls. Create the game board out of a large cardboard box with ready-made dividers, or make your own dividers by taping poster board pieces to the inside of the box in a grid pattern. Label each section with a single-digit number, in any order. To play, divide the class into two teams. Have the first student throw the balls into the box. He or she must add, subtract, multiply, or divide the two digits where the balls land, depending on the skill and level you desire. If the student answers correctly, the team gets a point. For more advanced students, require players to correctly complete all four computations in order to earn points for each of their teams.
—*Shawn Stillway, Bridgeport, CT*

Science Carnival

In my second-grade classroom, our class holds a Science Carnival before we begin each unit. I set up discovery stations around the room for student groups to rotate among and experience. I usually introduce each station by acting like a ringmaster, and saying (in a loud, deep voice), "And in this corner...." Students munch on popcorn as we read aloud about the upcoming unit. This introduction really adds to the carnival atmosphere, and gets the children ready and excited to proceed.
—*Leanne Phelps, Broken Arrow, OK*

Classroom Continents

When teaching land forms to my third graders, I arrange their desks into seven groups, each labeled as a different continent. I also put masking tape through the center of our "desk map" to symbolize the equator. They learn first-hand which countries are to the north or south of the equator, concepts that are sometimes difficult for children to grasp from a flat map. We also discuss the varying climates of different countries due to their proximities to the equator. To teach longitude, I later change our tape line to the prime meridian.
—*Kim Land, Muskogee, OK*

Poetry Break! In my third-grade classroom, I created a stop sign out of red construction paper taped to a ruler, with the words "Poetry Break" on it. During our poetry unit, students can sign up for a turn to "stop" the class, and then share a poem that they have been practicing reading aloud with expression. This idea has worked wonderfully. My students love stopping the class by holding up the sign and calling out "Stop! Poetry Break!" whenever they are ready. I have found that enthusiasm for sharing poetry increases even with the most reluctant readers in my class. —*Kara Baker, Airdrie, Alberta, Canada*

Congressional Mobiles

To help students learn about our two-chamber legislative branch of government, give each small group a wire hanger. Ask each group to label two tagboard shapes "Senate" and "House of Representatives," and use colored string to affix to its hanger. Students next write out the respective qualifications and duties of senators and representatives on tagboard shapes, and attach the lists below the correct chamber. Add photos and details for each of your state's current senators and representatives.
— *Cindy Woolston, Brunswick, MO*

Campfire Tales

Make the diversity of the American West come alive. Invite students to develop their own characters from history to share at a classroom "camp-fire" party.

To begin, share excerpts from books on the 1800s. Have students each choose a fictional or historical character or invent one inspired by their reading. Then ask students to write in the voices of their characters a short story, poem, newspaper article, song, journal entry, or letter. Plan a special day for students to bring in props and wear costumes to represent their characters. Gather around a construction-paper campfire and let students tell, sing, or read their writings. Who will visit your camp? A pioneer girl traveling along the Oregon Trail? An Arapaho boy on his first buffalo hunt? An African-American cowboy? A Chinese railroad worker? A mountain man? — *Mary Lotzer, Lauderdale, MN*

Postmark Graphing

For a fun math and geography review during the fall and winter holiday seasons, start a class postmark collection. Display a large wall map of the United States, and encourage students to bring in as many postmarks as they can find. Have them cut out and attach these to the map on the appropriate states with removable adhesive. Then, each day, ask students to tally the number of postmarks in each state. Later, invite students to graph the data. — *Denise Wadas, Wichita, KS*

Lego® Archaeology

Just because something is in print does not make it accurate. Ideas change as new information is uncovered, and different people may interpret the same information in different ways. To reinforce these concepts with your older students, try a round of Lego Archaeology. Purchase several small, identical sets of Lego building blocks and put each set into a plastic bag, with all instructions and pictures removed. Divide the class into small groups, and tell students that each group is now a team of scientists from another planet studying an archaeological site on a planet called Earth. Using its assigned bag of "artifacts," each team must determine what the object might have been and then try to assemble it. Usually no two groups will put the pieces together in the same way!
— *Dorothy Hill, Potts Camp, MS*

Assembled by Group 2

Assembled by Group 1

FABULOUS FALL FUN

Bring the rich colors of autumn into your classroom with festive folk art! By Mackie Rhodes

PAINT

CUT

STUFF

DECORATE

Bag-o'-Lanterns

This clever craft will get a glowing review when students use their lanterns for counting practice or to set up and solve simple math problems.

For each lantern you'll need a paper lunch bag, orange and green paint, yellow tissue paper, green and black construction paper, glue, scissors, and green pipe cleaners.

Set up a painting station, then guide students through these steps:

1. Slip a bag over your hand and evenly paint it orange. Let dry.

2. Flatten the bag and fold it in half, as shown. Starting at the fold, cut slits lengthwise through all layers of the bag. Be sure to stop cutting about an inch from the end opposite the fold.

3. Carefully open the bag and set upright. Stuff gently with loosely crumpled tissue paper.

4. Twist the top of the bag closed and paint the twist green to make a stem. Set aside to dry.

5. Use curled pipe cleaners to attach leaves cut from green construction paper to top of bag.

6. Create unique jack-o'-lantern faces by glueing on features cut from black construction paper.

For spooky seasonal displays, hang the lanterns from the ceiling around your classroom.

—Adapted from ideas by Sue DeRiso, Barrington, RI, and Susan Bunyan, Dodge City, KS

Nocturnal Animal Masks

Complement a fall lesson on nocturnal animals with fun hand-made owl and raccoon masks.

For each mask you'll need a paper plate, the **Reproducible** (opposite), construction paper, glue, scissors, and string. Give each child a plate and a copy of the reproducible, and then guide students through the following steps:

❶ Cut a construction paper circle (in a color such as yellow, black, or orange) and glue to the center of your plate.

❷ Trace the owl or raccoon eye-mask pattern onto construction paper and glue to the plate. Cut out the eye holes.

❸ Trace additional features from the reproducible onto construction paper. Cut and glue into place on your mask.

❹ Staple a length of string to each side of your mask.

Wear masks during read alouds of favorite owl and raccoon books, such as *Owl Moon*, by Jane Yolen (Philomel, 1987) or *Timothy Goes to School*, by Rosemary Wells (Puffin, 2000).

Miniature Scarecrow

These cornfield friends make great fall reading buddies!

For each scarecrow you'll need a single-size cereal box, a 3" Styrofoam ball, construction paper, two googly eyes, a craft stick, paint, yarn, glue, and scissors.

Guide students through these steps:

1. Stuff your empty box with paper and glue it closed. Paint and let dry.

2. Poke one end of the craft stick into the Styrofoam ball. Paint yellow and let dry.

3. Cut a slit in one end of the box. Insert the craft stick to attach scarecrow's head.

4. For arms and legs, accordion-fold construction paper strips and glue onto box.

5. Glue on paper hands and feet, googly eyes, and yarn or raffia to resemble hair.

6. Add other features using cut paper, paint, or craft items such as buttons.

—Adapted from an idea by Suzanne Moore, Irving, TX

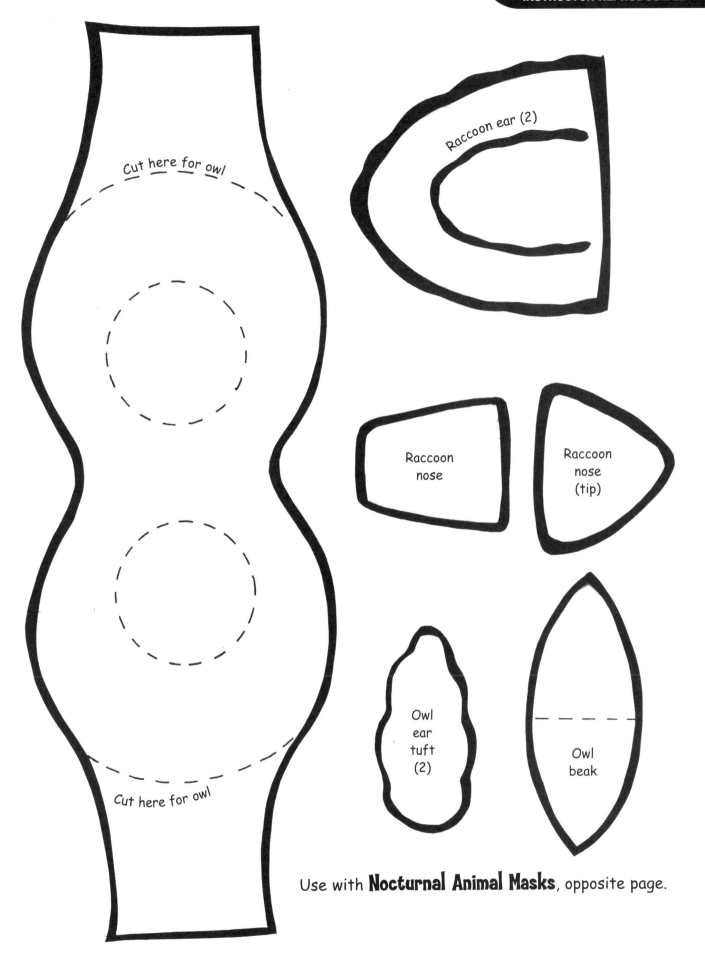

Cut here for owl

Raccoon ear (2)

Raccoon nose

Raccoon nose (tip)

Owl ear tuft (2)

Owl beak

Cut here for owl

Use with **Nocturnal Animal Masks**, opposite page.

Hoot, Hoot, Hooray!
An Owls Theme Unit
By Mackie Rhodes

Students will hoot over these owl-related activities and become all the wiser as they learn about our fascinating feathered friends. Plus: A fun-filled reproducible page!

Observe, Wonder, Learn

Display a variety of owl pictures, books, and other resources around your classroom. Then create a three-column chart that can guide your students' learning.

Use the chart to help your class organize its owl observations, questions, and new knowledge. Encourage students to continue to add to the chart as they learn more about owls throughout the unit.

Wise About Size

Size up students' owl knowledge with this fact-filled display. First, have pairs of students research an owl of their choice, using books such as *All About Owls*, by Jim Arnosky (Scholastic, 1999) or *The Book of North American Owls*, by Helen Roney Sattler (Houghton Mifflin, 1998). Encourage children to draw life-sized pictures of their owls. Have them label speech-bubble cutouts with owl facts written from their owls' perspectives, such as "I hunt my prey only at night." To display, ask

students to sequence the owls' sizes, label each with its name and height, and add its speech bubble. Invite students to share their owls with the class. Discuss the difference in size and characteristics of different owl species.

From Egg to Independence

Use information from *The Barn Owl*, by Sally Tagholm (Kingfisher, 1999), and other resources to design a class time line that describes an owl's development from new chick to independent owlet. Afterward, ask children to imagine they are newly-hatched chicks—perhaps the oldest, middle, or youngest of several chicks or even the only owlet in the nest. Ask your young "owls" to write journals about their observations, development, and experi-

Learn How Baby Birds Survive

Divide the class into five "nests" of birds, and elect a parent bird for each. Give the parent one of the following beaks: chopsticks, tweezers, a plastic fork, or a toothpick. (The baby birds each get a small paper cup.) Set out a few plates of treats: gummy worms, raisins, etc. Within a set time limit, the mother birds fly out and pluck as many treats as they can with their beaks, delivering them to the chirping baby birds' cups in the nest. Ask students to consider which beaks work best for certain types of food.
—*Denise Bryan, Plymouth-Canton Community Schools, Plymouth, MI*

ences from the day they emerge from their eggs to Independence Day, when they leave the nest.

Sight, Sound, Flight, Found!

Experience how owls use their eyes, ears, wings, and talons with this activity. Appoint several children to be owls, and send them out of the room. Then place assorted plastic animals or other "owl prey" around the room. Station children near each animal and designate a particular noise for each one. Dim or turn off the lights. Then have the owls return to sit on an imaginary perch in the center of the room. To play, one owl at a time searches for prey by peering out from its perch until it hears the quiet noise of an animal (secretly made by a child on cue). Then the owl "flies" toward the noise. When it locates the animal,

the owl grasps it in its talons and flies back to the nest to feast. After all the owls have caught their prey, have children switch roles and play again.

Trick...or Treat?

When danger approaches, an owl senses that it's trick-or-treat time—it must either escape an enemy attack with a bit of trickery or become a tasty treat! Some owls play dead to trick the enemy, while others fluff out their feathers, spread their wings, clack their beaks, and hiss to appear large and tough. Some act injured to lead the enemy away from their young, then fly to safety. Others throw their voices like ventriloquists. One owl can even imitate a rattlesnake sound. For some trick-or-treat fun, invite students to create owl masks to wear while role-playing a variety of owl tricks. ■

Cool Collage Owls

Wrap up your unit with these cool critters (**Reproducible**, page 24). Ask students to label the parts of their owls and share their collages and owl knowledge with their families.

To Make a Collage Owl:

❶ Make copies of the **Reproducible** on page 24 for each student. Have students cut out the shapes and trace them on construction paper. Ask them to fold a piece of paper in half, then trace and cut out the wing shape to make two matching wings.

❷ To make each eye, trace the larger oval onto orange or yellow paper and then glue the smaller oval in the center.

❸ Trace the diamond shape onto yellow construction paper and fold it in half to make a beak.

❹ Glue the eyes, wings, and the fold of the beak onto the owl's body.

❺ To make the owl's feathers, tear a newspaper into 2-inch strips, and glue them on in overlapping rows.

—From *Art Projects That Dazzle and Delight,* by Karen Backus (Scholastic, 2002).

Pick a Pellet Apart

Examining the contents of owl pellets can provide students with interesting information about owl diets, as well as their prey. But where do you find owl pellets? Simply go to www.pellet lab.com or www.pelletsinc.com to order online. Or order by phone from Carolina Biological Supply Company (1-800-334-5551). For the faint of heart, www.kidwings.com takes visitors through a virtual hands-off owl-pellet dissection.

Use with **Cool Collage Owls**, page 23.

MULTIPLICATION MYSTERIES

Treat students to fun on Halloween as they practice their multiplication "tricks"
By Jodi Simpson

Mystery Mansion

Boo! How many legs, wings, hands, eyes, and teeth belong to the creatures in the Mystery Mansion? Let your students practice problem solving and multiplication with a lift-the-flap pair of reproducibles. First, pass out the **Reproducibles** on pages 26 and 27 and have your students cut out and color the mansion and creatures. Each square containing a set of creatures will become a window flap on the mansion. Have children use clear tape to affix the top of each square to the top of a window. To calculate the features on each creature, children lift the flap to reveal the word problem underneath. Give children time to solve the problems on scratch paper. When the problems are solved, they can write their answers as equations on a separate sheet (for example, 6 x 2 = 12).

Candy Corn Calculations

Invite your students to have fun practicing their multiplication in a tasty, hands-on way. Use this activity for children to "see" their multiplication tables as they create sets of candy corn to solve their own products. First, divide your class into groups of two; provide each group with a pair of dice and 40 pieces of candy corn. One child will roll one die to represent the number of sets of candy the pair will make. The other child will roll the second die to find out how many pieces of corn will be in each set. For example, one child might roll a 6 while his or her partner rolls a 5. Together, the children arrange the factors they've rolled (6 sets of 5 pieces of candy corn, or 6 x 5 = 30). Circulate around the room to help kids find their factors, multipliers, and products.

For Older Students: Those ready for work with larger numbers can use playing cards instead of dice. Remove the face cards from a standard deck and provide partners with the Ace through 10 cards. To play, each child chooses a card to find the factors.

Mystery Trick-or-Treat Bag

Have students reach into the trick-or-treat bag to pull out a mystery! Provide pairs of children with paper bags with "Trick or Treat" written on them. Then, pass out scraps of paper on which they can copy the numbered problems below before placing the problems in their bags. Next, ask each pair to grab and solve a problem, writing out their thinking, factors, and products.

1. Five children each got six candies. How many pieces did they have all together?
2. Seven witches lost their pointed shoes in a ditch. How many shoes did they search for?
3. Four scarecrows needed gloves. How many gloves did they need in total?
4. Three monsters got eight stitches each. How many stitches did they get in all?
5. Six goblins each ate three caramel apples. All together, how many apples did they eat?
6. Three ghosts came home with eleven lollipops each. How many did they have?

Bat Wing Stew

Distribute the **Reproducible** on page 26. Students multiply the various ingredients to convert the given recipe into an equivalent recipe, writing their answers in the blanks. They can then make up their own recipes for classmates to solve.

Multiplication Links

Multiplication Flash Card Practice
www.surfnetkids.com/games/multiplication-fc.htm
Play timed 30-second flashcard games.

Multiplication Matching Game
http://kidshub.org/kids/multiplication.cfm
Click on a problem and then its solution in this interactive game.

Multiplication Games
www.primaryresources.co.uk/online/moonmaths.swf
Click an alien to solve the problem.

Use with **Mystery Mansion**, opposite page. Activity on page 25.

Directions:
Color and carefully cut out the pieces. Then use a small piece of clear tape to attach the top of the piece to the top of the correct window on the Mystery Mansion, opposite. Lift the flaps and solve the problems!

Use with **Bat Wing Stew**, page 25.

Directions: Use your multiplication skills to solve the creepy crawly problems below. (Example: 6 monsters x 3 eyes = how many monster eyes?) Then write the answers in the blanks on the "Bat Wing Stew" recipe card at right.

- The eyes of 6 three-eyed monsters
- The rattle of 1 rattlesnake
- The legs of 8 lizards
- The legs of 9 spiders
- The wings of 7 bats
- The juice of 10 half-cups of pond water

Bat Wing Stew

By the light of a full moon, bring to a bubbling boil the following delectable ingredients:

_____ monster eyes

_____ rattlesnake rattle(s)

_____ lizard legs

_____ spider legs

_____ bat wings

_____ cups of pond water

ANSWERS ON PAGE 2.

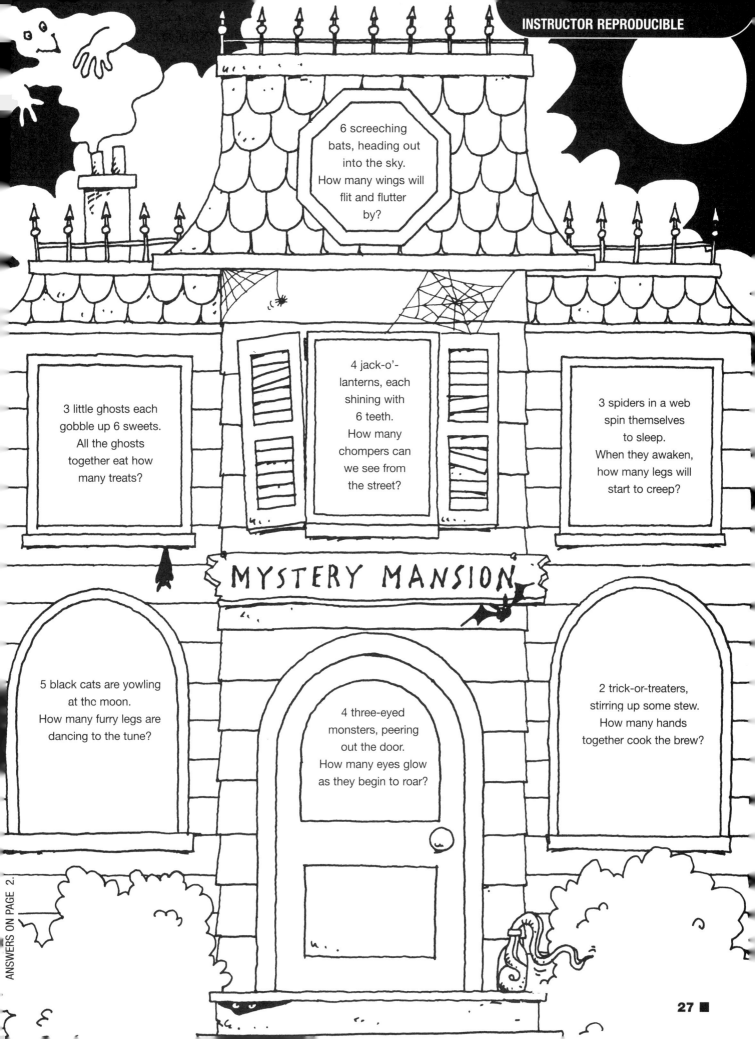

6 screeching bats, heading out into the sky. How many wings will flit and flutter by?

3 little ghosts each gobble up 6 sweets. All the ghosts together eat how many treats?

4 jack-o'-lanterns, each shining with 6 teeth. How many chompers can we see from the street?

3 spiders in a web spin themselves to sleep. When they awaken, how many legs will start to creep?

MYSTERY MANSION

5 black cats are yowling at the moon. How many furry legs are dancing to the tune?

4 three-eyed monsters, peering out the door. How many eyes glow as they begin to roar?

2 trick-or-treaters, stirring up some stew. How many hands together cook the brew?

INTO THE BAT CAVE

Engage students in high-flying science learning with these creatures of the night   **By Starin Lewis**

Bats 101

Are you afraid of bats? Well, did you know that bats are afraid of you? These amazing mammals have long been misunderstood! In fact, bats actually help the environment and people by eating tons of flying insects that destroy crops and spread diseases. Bats also pollinate night flowers, such as cactus, and help spread seeds to create new fruit trees. Begin your science study—just in time for the Halloween season—by immersing students in learning about bats. Provide them with fiction and nonfiction books, poetry, magazines, videos, Web sites, and other media. Then invite students to create a class KWL chart decorated with bat die-cuts. Building up students' background knowledge first will make their use of the chart richer. After reading about bats and viewing some photographs, ask students, "What do you now know about these animals?" and "What else do you want to know?" Refer to the chart often during your unit; as students find the answers to their questions, invite them to add their knowledge to the "learned" column.

Did You Know?

- Bats are the only mammals that can fly.
- Bats are *nocturnal*, or active at night.
- Bats live in forests, deserts, and cities.
- The smallest bat is the size of an insect.
- The largest bat has a wingspan of 6 feet.
- Bats hang upside down to rest or sleep.
- Bats can fly as fast as 60 miles per hour.

Going Batty

The structure of a bat is unique. Help your class understand bat anatomy in a fun way by inviting them to dress as bats. Each student will need a bath towel and two small sandwich bags to simulate both the span and transparency of a bat's wings. Explain that a bat's wing doesn't have feathers, like a bird's does; it is actually made of thin, tough, and semi-translucent skin. Have students drape their towels around their shoulders and put their hands into the bags. Since bats use their thumbs—which stick out from their wings—to grab onto walls and trees, have students push their thumbs through the bags. Explain that bats come in different colors and patterns (brown, gray, black, red, frosted, spotted, etc.), just as students' towels may look different. In order to fly, a bat moves its wings in the same way a person would swim the butterfly stroke. Have students practice this maneuver by "flying" around the room. Then tell students that, when bats sleep, they wrap their wings around themselves and hang upside down. Have students wrap their arms close to their bodies and pretend to sleep.

Home Sweet Home

Bats live in all kinds of homes: Caves, barns, tall trees, attics, and garages are some of their favorite roosting spots. After discussing these habitats with your class, invite small groups of students each to choose a favorite bat habitat and create a diorama of it. Provide cardboard boxes and art materials such as construction paper, paint, markers, crayons, glue, tape, and fishing line or yarn. For the bats, students can use their own drawings or cutouts from the **Reproducible** on page 30. As groups plan their models, encourage them to use the backs and outsides of their boxes as well as the insides. For example, if students chose a barn as their habitat, they could paint the back of the box like the front of a barn. Viewers will see the front of the barn and be able to turn it around to see inside, too. Encourage each group to present its diorama and include facts about the bats inside it.

The Benefits of Bats

Bats have an image problem. Most people think they are aggressive or dirty animals. In fact, bats are nature's exterminators because they eat so many insects and other pests. Bats are also nature's farmers; without  bats, many plants would not be pollinated to grow new plants, and fruit-bearing trees would not produce nearly as many new trees. Encourage your class to educate people about the benefits of bats. Start a campaign by making posters, buttons, and bumper stickers to promote a positive view of bats. You could even invite students to give public-service announcements over the school loudspeaker or write editorials for the paper.

Echo! Location!

Have you ever wondered how bats are able to hunt for food at night when it is dark? Scientists have discovered that bats use *echolocation* to find their prey. When a bat is flying, it makes a series of high-pitched squeaks that humans can't hear. The sounds hit an object and bounce back to the bat, like an echo. The bat is able to tell the size and distance of the object just from the echo. This allows the bat to lock in on its prey, swoop down, and catch it. Give students a chance to practice their own echolocation. Choose one student to be the "bat," and blindfold him or her. Arrange the other students in a circle around the bat, and select another student in the circle to be the bat's "prey." Ask the bat to call out "echo" from the center of the circle. The prey should respond "location." The bat continues to say "echo," moving slowly toward the location of the prey. Once the bat has found the prey, he or she stops and takes off the blindfold. Allow other students to take turns at being the bat or the prey.

Becoming "Bat-ologists"

Bats eat a variety of food. Although a few drink the blood of livestock, most eat fruit, insects, and fish. Tell students that they are going to be zookeepers in charge of a bat exhibit for the day. An important part of this job is to plan meals for the bats. Divide the class into small groups. Assign a few different bats to each group, such as the vampire bat, flying fox bat, bumblebee bat, big-eared bat, bulldog bat, and little brown bat. Have each group research what its bats eat and look like. Then encourage students to create menu posters to share their findings with the class. Students in each group can work together to draw pictures of their bats, or find photographs on the Web or in magazines. Below these images, they can draw or glue cutouts of the foods they've selected for each bat.

The Genuine Article

There are more than 1,000 species of bats in the world, and all of them are fascinating. Invite your class to put together a class magazine to share their knowledge about these intriguing creatures. Ask each student to choose a bat to research in depth using books, Web sites, and the library. Encourage students to find photographs of their chosen bats. Next, have small groups of students each cut apart one or more 8 ½" x 11" sheets of 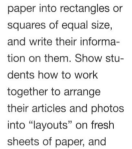 paper into rectangles or squares of equal size, and write their information on them. Show students how to work together to arrange their articles and photos into "layouts" on fresh sheets of paper, and paste in place to create a complete page. Gather all the pages and bind into your magazine of the "coolest" bats in the world. ■

Bat Resources

Bats *By Adrienne Mason (Kids Can Press, 2003).* This detailed yet easy-to-read book is packed with accurately illustrated information, plus a glossary of terms.

Bats (Grades 1–3): Complete Cross-Curricular Theme Unit *By Robin Bernard (Scholastic, 1998).* Includes reproducibles, activities, and a full-color poster.

Zipping, Zapping, Zooming Bats *By Ann Earle (HarperTrophy, 1995).* A great general overview of bats and their behavior, plus ecology and conservation information.

Bat Conservation International www.batcon.org
A great place to learn about the value of bats! Includes extensive links to education sites on bats.

BATS CHALLENGE

Directions: Cut out each black fact-square below and paste it on the matching bat card. Bonus: Put two sets together and play "Concentration."

Flying Fox Bat

paste
square here

Bumblebee Bat

paste
square here

Vampire Bat

paste
square here

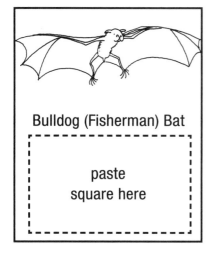

Bulldog (Fisherman) Bat

paste
square here

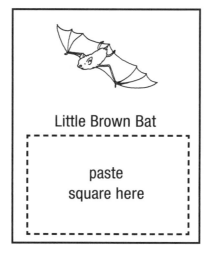

Little Brown Bat

paste
square here

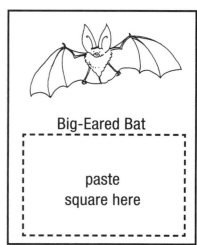

Big-Eared Bat

paste
square here

This tiny bat is the smallest kind of bat in the world.

This bat looks like a rabbit with its big ears and nose.

This bat uses its fangs to feed on cows, pigs, and mules.

This plain brown bat is the most common bat in the United States.

This giant, fluffy bat has a face that makes it look like a fox.

This bat swoops out of the sky and catches fish for its dinner.

ANSWERS ON PAGE 2.

NOT-SO-SCARY STORYBOOK OCTOBER

Put a literary twist on the season of bats, ghosts, and pumpkins

By Lucia Kemp Henry

Reading Response Journals

Invite students to get the most from seasonal books with reading response journals. Give students each a 9" x 12" piece of construction paper and about a dozen sheets of 6" x 9" lined paper. Show them how to fold the construction paper in half to make front and back booklet covers, insert the lined paper, and staple together along the fold. Each child can title his or her booklet (e.g. "Halloween Reading Journal"), then decorate the cover. Encourage students to record their reactions and ideas after each independent reading session. You might also host special Halloween reading time. Ask students to bring in small flashlights, and set the mood with a recording of a thunderstorm at low volume. Light candles or a jack-o'-lantern, and have children read by the glow of their flashlights. Later, ask students to write in their journals about how the spooky environment enriched their reading experiences.

Story Setting Read Aloud

Focus on setting as an important story element by selecting a favorite read-aloud passage that describes a place. For example, the third chapter of *Harry Potter and the Sorcerer's Stone* (Scholastic, 1999) describes the gloomy, sea-battered, storm-shattered shack where Harry and the Dursleys stay. As you read, have students close their eyes and listen carefully for descriptive words and phrases. Afterwards, prompt them to recall some of the language the author used and list their responses on chart paper. Then ask each child, guided by the chart, to draw his or her own picture of the same scene and a few sentences describing the drawing. When completed, use the pictures to prompt a discussion of how each listener interprets the scene differently.

A Dark and Stormy Night

Challenge students to create their own suspenseful settings, inspired by the vivid descriptions in many tales of the season. Begin by having students suggest word categories, such as time of day and year, weather, place, sound, and smell. Use chalk to write the categories each on a black cloud-shaped piece of construction paper. Add a yellow paper lightening bolt to each cloud, then glue the clouds to separate columns on bulletin board paper. Ask students to brainstorm a list of words for each category. Then have them use the words to write descriptive paragraphs that begin "It was a dark and stormy night ..." ■

My Favorite Great Halloween Read

Great October Reads

Mysterious characters and seasonal critters are a must when students are choosing a great seasonal read. Encourage independent reading by providing a suitable list of recommended titles. Then ask each student to select a book with a favorite creepy character, a fall theme, or one that focuses on seasonal creatures such as bats, owls, or spiders. When students have chosen, have each complete the **Reproducible** on page 32, naming a favorite book and why he or she would recommend it to a classmate. After students have decorated and cut out their pumpkins, display on a seasonal bulletin board. Extend the activity by having children discuss their choices in small groups.

Name _____

Use with
Great October Reads, page 31.

Title:

Author:

Why I like this book:

Explorers
of the Americas

Send your students on an imaginary stow-away adventure By Jacqueline Clarke

Give your explorers unit a twist and watch students' interest take off. Working in groups, students research and write a first-hand record of an explorer's voyage as if they were stowing away on a journey across the sea.

Trip Trackers

Begin with some preliminary research as a class. Study and compare the journeys and routes of major explorers to the New World. Cover your world map with clear laminate and draw the route of each explorer you study. Make a key with a different symbol and color for each explorer. As a class, compare their routes, distances, travel dates, and discoveries. Who traveled the farthest? Who made the most discoveries? Then challenge students with the map Reproducible on page 34.

Explorer Time Line Posters

Divide the class into groups and let each group choose an explorer with whom to "travel." One good place to start is ThinkQuest Junior Explorer's time line site (http://tqjunior.think quest.org/4034/timeline2.html). On poster board, have each group record their explorer's dates of exploration and discoveries. Suggest they add a few stowaway touches such as "Our hiding place was nearly discovered today!" Invite the groups to decorate their

posters with their own illustrations of the voyage. Hang the posters around the room and encourage students to look for similarities and differences, such as which countries sponsored the voyage and what the explorers' goals were.

Postcards From Stowaways

Ask each "stowaway" to record his or her journey on a postcard addressed to a friend or family member. They can write, for example, about the day they set sail, the experience of a storm at sea, or the first time they saw land. Encourage them to use their imaginations and their creative skills, drawing or tracing their own illustrations for the postcards. Share the postcards by reading them aloud and by having

students exchange and answer each others' postcards.

Interview the Stowaways

Celebrate the end of their hard work and research by inviting the groups of stowaways to take turns sharing "actual" stories of their adventures and days with a famous explorer over mugs of frosty root beer. They can dress up in big boots, eye patches, or floppy hats with feathers. For simple props, try construction-paper telescopes, drawings of their explorers' ships, or hand-decorated handkerchief nautical flags. The rest of the class can act as news reporters asking questions of the adventurers: What was the best thing they learned? Where would they like to explore next? ■

Books to Explore

● *Explorer,* by Rupert Matthews (Dorling Kindersley, 2003)
● *You Are the Explorer,* by Nathan Aaseng (Oliver, 1999)
● *Explor-a-Maze,* by Robert Snedden (Millbrook, 1998)
● *The Discovery of the Americas,* by Betsy and Giulio Maestro (HarperCollins, 1991)

Links to Explore

● Gander Academy Explorers site: www.stemnet.nf.ca/CITE/explorer.htm?
● European explorers crossword puzzle: http://library.thinkquest.org/ J002678F/explorers_crossword_puz zle.htm?tqskip1=1
● Peek into Christopher Columbus's journal at www.fordham.edu/halsall /source/columbus1.html

Special thanks to the teachers who contributed their ideas: Bob Krech, Janet Worthington-Samo, and Judy Wetzel.

Name _____

Meet the
EXPLORERS

Directions: Answer each question with the name of the correct explorer.

1. I believe I discovered the New World first in 1001 A.D.

_____

2. In 1492, I set sail with the Niña, the Pinta, and the Santa Maria.

_____

3. I was the first explorer to circumnavigate the globe, in 1577.

_____

4. I journeyed to Florida in search of the Fountain of Youth.

_____

5. I traveled to and claimed Newfoundland for England.

_____

6. I named the Pacific Ocean for its peaceful waves.

_____

ANSWERS ON PAGE 2.

Mayflower Math

Voyage into history and math with our shipshape Thanksgiving theme unit,
featuring a two-page Mayflower reproducible **By Jacqueline Clarke**

On September 6, 1620, 102 passengers boarded a 90-foot boat and traveled 3,500 nautical miles over 66 days to find a new home. Help students make important math connections as they learn about this fascinating *Mayflower* voyage!

Before You Begin
Gather books about the Pilgrims and the *Mayflower* voyage and bookmark relevant Web sites for your students to investigate and explore.

Begin by giving the *Mayflower* **Reproducible** on page 36 to your students and having them make ship's logs (see below). Explain that this drawing is called a "cutaway" because one side is

removed, enabling us to see the inside. As you review the key to different areas of the ship, have your students make a list of questions and things they want to learn about the voyage. Using questions in this unit and those from students, write a new challenge on a sentence strip each day and post it for students to answer.

How Many Children Sailed on the *Mayflower*?
A surprising number of children emigrated on the Pilgrim ship, nearly one third of all passengers. Give each student 32 beans to represent the Pilgrim children and have them use the diagram as a math mat to solve the following problems:

● How many people are pictured in the *Mayflower* diagram? How many more passengers were there?

● When the weather was calm, children could run free on the upper deck. If 13 children were above deck, how many were below deck?

● Most of the passengers slept "tween decks." Some slept in the shallop. Divide the children evenly among these two spaces.

● There were no bathrooms on the *Mayflower*. Washing was done with seawater up on deck. If 9 children rose early to wash, how many were still sleeping?

● There were 21 boys on the ship. How many girls? Help students to calculate the ratio of boys to girls in their ship's logs. How does the ratio compare with the numbers in your class?

Extend your activities on the *Mayflower* children by making paper dolls to decorate your classroom and use in counting and dramatic play. You can learn the names and histories of the Pilgrim boys and girls at www.mayflowerhistory.com

How Big Was the Ship?
Compared with ships today, the *Mayflower* wasn't overly large. In their ship's logs, let students calculate and record the length of the ship's hull using the scale on the reproducible. Help students compare the size of the ship with other spaces. *(Continued on page 38)*

2-page repro on page 36

Super Ship's Logs • Up in the "round house" Captain Jones charted the progress of the *Mayflower* in a ship's log. Let students create their own ship's logs as they embark on this mathematical journey. Copy the *Mayflower* Reproducible onto 11" x 18" sheets of paper to create covers. Place the diagram on top of several blank sheets and fasten together with a brad. Tape feathers to the ends of children's pencils to simulate the quill pens used in Colonial times. Use these logs to pose questions, record research, and solve math problems.

The Mayflower, 1620

A sailing ship meant to carry cargo, the Mayflower left Plymouth, England, carrying 30 sailors and 102 Pilgrims, including 32 children, to voyage to America.

A **Mast** made from a strong tree, supports the ship and sails

B **Round House** where charts were kept and the ship's course plotted

C **Great Cabin** where the captain slept

D **Steerage** where sailors steered, using a tiller and compass

E **'Tween Decks** where the Pilgrims ate and slept

F **Fo'C'Sle** (FOLK-sill) where the crew's meals were cooked

G **Hold** where the supplies were stored

H **Gun Room** where guns and ammunition were stored

I **Shallop** a small boat used for exploring and for going ashore

J **Windlass** a simple machine used to lift the ship's anchor

K **Ballast** rocks that helped to keep the ship stable

L **Deck** the top open-air level of the ship

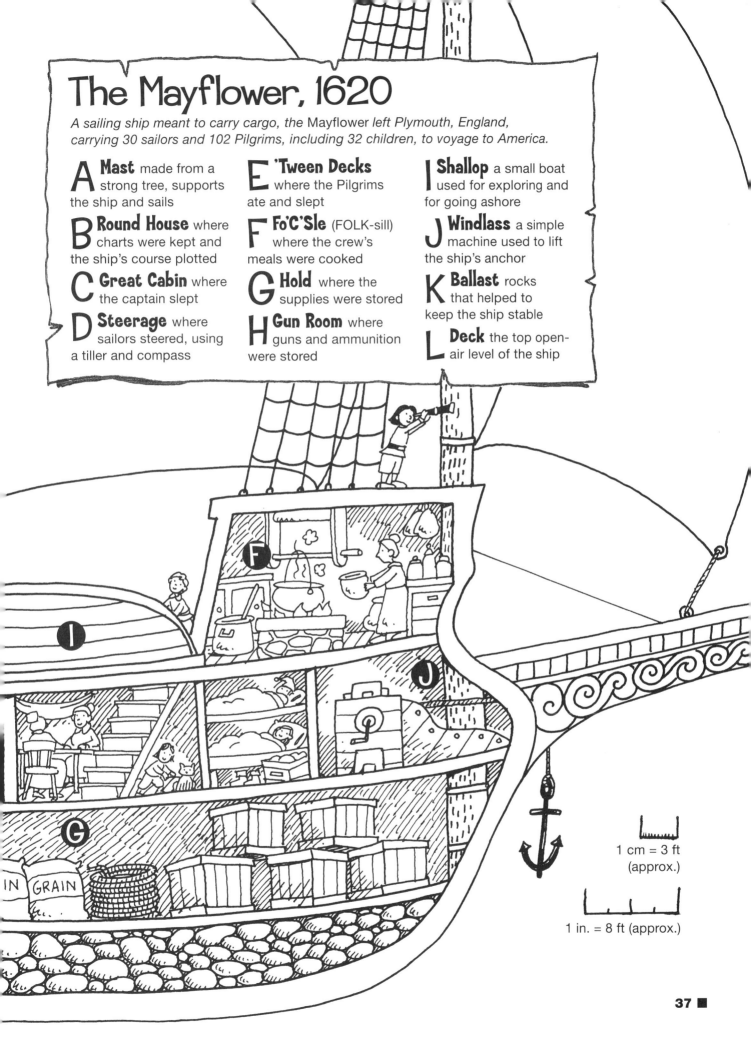

1 cm = 3 ft (approx.)

1 in. = 8 ft (approx.)

(*Continued from page 35*)
● Measure the length of your classroom. Is it larger than the *Mayflower*?
● Measure the length of the school parking lot. How many *Mayflower* ships could fit along its length?
● Measure the length of the school gymnasium. Find the difference between its measurement and the *Mayflower*.

How Long Was the Voyage?

For the passengers aboard the *Mayflower*, the time passed slowly. They read books and sang songs, but the harsh conditions made it difficult to endure. Finally, after two months at sea, they reached land. Copy the Voyage Time Line (at right) on the board, or make copies to give to your students as bookmarks.
● How many days passed before land was sighted? How many more days did it take for the ship to reach land?
● The *Mayflower* passengers and crew spent 66 days at sea. Convert this number into weeks and minutes.
● How many days have you been in school this year? Is the number greater or less than 66 days?

● During which season did the colonists spend their first night in Plymouth? Why might this have been difficult for them?
● The *Mayflower* set sail for Plymouth, England, on April 5, 1621. How long had it been away?

Mayflower Word Problems

End your mathematical journey with one last entry in your ship's log! Challenge each student to compose his or her own word problems based on mathematical data collected during the "trip." Invite students to exchange papers and use their "quill pens" to solve each other's problems. ▥

SHIP-TO-SHORE READ ALOUDS
● *Eating the Plates: A Pilgrim Book of Food and Manners*, by Lucille Recht Penner (Aladdin, 1997).
● *On the Mayflower: Voyage of the Ship's Apprentice and a Passenger Girl*, by Kate Waters (Scholastic, 1996).
● *If You Sailed on the Mayflower in 1620*, by Ann McGovern (Scholastic, 1993).

What Did the Pilgrims Eat?

Can you imagine eating the same food every day? One of the staples in the Pilgrims' diet was hardtack, a dry, hard biscuit made from flour and water. If possible, make hardtack and do a taste test and some recipe math with your students. Begin by having students copy the hardtack recipe into their ship's logs and record their impressions. Use the hardtack as edible (sort of!) manipulatives as you pose math questions to your class. Example: If the 32 children on the *Mayflower* each ate two biscuits per day, how many would they eat altogether?

Recipe for Hardtack

INGREDIENTS: 3 cups flour, 1 cup plus 1 tablespoon water
DIRECTIONS: 1. Preheat oven to 450°.
2. Add water to the flour and mix thoroughly. Knead and punch dough for 10 minutes.

3. Roll out the dough (about 1 inch thickness) and cut with biscuit cutter.
4. Place biscuits on a cookie sheet and prick a few times with a fork.
5. Bake for 7 minutes. Turn down the oven to 350° and bake for an additional 7–10 minutes. Makes 2 dozen.

Mayflower Voyage Time Line

September 6, 1620
Mayflower leaves Plymouth, England.

November 9, 1620
Cape Cod sighted.

November 11, 1620
Mayflower lands at Cape Cod; Mayflower Compact signed.

November 28, 1620
Captain Standish and others explore coast in a shallop.

December 20, 1620
Colonists spend first night in Plymouth.

April 5, 1621
Mayflower returns to Plymouth, England.

Winter

Standards-Based Activities

Practicing Measurement, Studying Ecosystems, Connecting Texts to Self and Others, Building Fluency, and Much More!

Winter ACTIVITIES
From Our Readers

Winter Sunshine Party A great activity to help get my second graders through the rainy and cold winter months is a sunshine party! Before the coldest weather sets in, we make "sunshine boxes" out of velum and take them outside to capture some sun and "charge" them. We sing "You Are My Sunshine" and invite the sunshine in. Then we hide all our individual sunshine boxes in a big yellow box. During February, we pull the boxes out from storage and host a party. We wear yellow clothing and eat yellow foods, and I even put hand warmers in yellow bean-bag material so we can feel the sun's warmth. The kids really love this and look forward to it all winter.
—*Trina Gunzel, Corvallis, OR*

Snow Day Stories To stir up some creativity on gray winter days, I invite my third graders to read Eric Carle's *Dream Snow* (Philomel, 2000), then write their own stories. **1.** They each choose a scene from their stories to brightly illustrate. **2.** I staple plastic transparency film over each picture, securing on one side. **3.** Students use white paint to create a blizzard scene on their overlays. Then they glue their story pages and snowy illustrations side by side on a large sheet of construction paper. Lifting each overlay reveals a before-and-after blizzard scene, just like in Carle's book.
—*Stephanie Scandalito, Fort Gratiot, MI*

Michelangelo Challenge Bring art history to life by giving students this hands-on Michelangelo challenge. After learning about Michelangelo's work on the Sistine Chapel, I encouraged my sixth graders to try creating original pictures while lying on their backs. Five minutes in, I heard choruses of "My arms are sore!" After struggling to completion, students shared their creations. We then discussed the challenges that they faced while painting. This activity gave them a greater appreciation for Michelangelo's work and talent.
—*Jennifer Boyce, Racine, WI*

Scribble Cookies Give new life to those small pieces of crayon piling up in your classroom by recycling them into Scribble Cookies. Remove any remaining paper labels and place the crayon scraps into a mini-muffin pan. Put the pan into a warm oven until the scraps melt into the muffin shapes, then let cool. When you pop them from the pan, each "cookie" will have a unique, colorful appearance, and can be used like a regular crayon.
—*Dr. Brad Wesner, Simpsonville, SC*

Frost-Making Magic

When you wake to find frost has covered the ground, that means the night temperature dropped below 0°C. Cold temperatures cause water vapor in the air to freeze instantly on surfaces such as grass or the top of a car. You can make frost happen inside the classroom to demonstrate this principle. Take an empty coffee can and fill it with ice and one-half cup of salt. Let students stir the ice and salt mixture with a spoon, and put on the lid. In just a few minutes, the can will be covered in frost!

Ice-Cube-Melting Race

Why does a lake often remain frozen, even though the temperature is above freezing? Simply put, it takes quite a lot of energy for ice to thaw, especially over a large surface. Show your students how much effort it takes to turn ice to water by having an ice-cube-melting race. Give each child a sealed zipper-style sandwich bag with an ice cube inside. Challenge them to come up with the quickest way to melt the ice cubes. They can try rubbing the bag, sitting on it, or blowing on it. Hint: The fastest way of melting ice is usually by smashing it, as the more surface area is in contact with the air, the faster it will melt.

Expanding Ice Trick

As water turns to ice, it expands as much as nine percent. This is why, when the temperature drops below 0°C, "frost wedging" can occur. Water trapped in tiny cracks expands, causing sidewalks to split and potholes to form. Show your students frost wedging in action with this experiment. Fill a plastic soda bottle to the brim, and screw the cap on tight. Place the bottle in a freezer overnight, and the next day you'll find that the bottle has split open. The ice has expanded outside the bottle!

Recycled Art Materials

Holiday-Box Dioramas
Old holiday-card boxes with clear plastic fronts make perfect mini-dioramas for kids to recreate favorite story scenes.

Easy Project Mats
Inexpensive dish drain boards make perfect art or project mats; try discount stores, or recycle them from parents!

Pizza-Box Portfolios
Ask a local pizza parlor to donate pizza boxes. Students can store projects and share work at a Portfolio Pizza Party.

Thanks to AnnMarie Stephens, Manassas, VA; Angela Gutteridge, Springfield, PA; and Heidi Gackenbach, Baltimore, MD, for these ideas!

Cold Water Sinks, Warm Water Rises

Why does lake water feel colder near the bottom than at the top? Sun and air help to warm the water near the surface. As water warms, it expands and becomes less dense—lighter. Cold water is denser and heavier. To demonstrate this, fill a large container half full with cold water, 12 ice cubes, and some blue food coloring. Stir to melt the ice. Fill an aquarium half full of warm water (about 50°C) and add red food coloring. Slowly pour the cold water down one side of the aquarium. You'll see the blue water sink to the bottom and form a layer under the warmer red water. How long do students predict it will take for the two waters to mix on their own, without stirring? *—All ice activities by Steve Tomecek*

SWEET

Get ready for the holiday season with crafts your students can share

Peppermint Candies

Turn your classroom into the "Land of Sweets" with these festive ceiling decorations. **For each decoration, you will need** two dessert-size paper plates, red markers or paint, pink plastic wrap or cellophane, and ribbon or yarn. Give each child two paper plates and then guide the class through the following steps:

1. Staple two paper plates together, top sides facing inward.
2. Using red markers or red paint, draw spirals or stripes on each side so the plate resembles a starlight mint.
3. Wrap the plates in pink cellophane and tie the ends with ribbon. Punch a hole in the top and hang from the ceiling with string or yarn.
    —*Kathy Cunningham, Morgan Road Elementary School, Liverpool, NY*

Peanut Butter Bird Feeders

These feeders make great gifts for winter birds! **To make the bird feeders, you will need** sliced bread, cookie cutters, craft sticks, peanut butter, sunflower seeds, sesame seeds, string or yarn, and scissors. Guide your class through the following steps:

1. Using cookie cutters, cut shapes from slices of soft white bread. Poke a small hole in the top of each one with a pencil. Let the bread shapes dry overnight.
2. The next day, when the bread is hard, use craft sticks to spread peanut butter on each shape. Sprinkle on the seeds.
3. Loop the string through the hole in the bread and tie it at the top. Hang these easy bird feeders outside your classroom window, or wrap them in foil for safe travel home.

Cool Cookie Jars

Practice measuring skills and more while making great holiday gifts—homemade cookies-to-go!
For each cookie jar, you will need a clean one-quart canning jar with a lid; a fabric square; the gift tag **Reproducible**, page 44; ribbon, scissors, and markers; and cookie ingredients. (For the full list of cookie ingredients, see the gift tag Reproducible. Set up your recipe-building station with clean jars, measuring implements, and containers filled with ingredients. Copy the recipe gift tags onto card stock for each student. Then guide students through the following directions:

1. Cut out and color the recipe gift tag on the Reproducible.
2. Measure each ingredient, layering them in order in your jar, one by one, following the recipe. As you add each layer, pack it down with a wooden spoon.
3. Twist the lid onto your jar. Then cover it with an 8" x 8" piece of fabric cut with scissors or pinking shears.
4. When your jar is done, return to your gift tag. On the inside of the tag, write a holiday greeting to your chosen recipient. Then, punch a hole through the tag and string ribbon through it. Tie the ribbon around the neck of the jar to hold the fabric in place. If unopened, your jar of yummy cookie ingredients will keep for two months, but you'll want cookies before then!
    —*Pat Resseguie and Joni Gray, Palmer Elementary School, Baldwinsville, NY*

CELEBRATIONS

Gingerbread People

These scented sandpaper gingerbread people smell almost as good as the real cookies do! For each student, you will need two squares of extra-fine sandpaper, a cinnamon stick, white fabric paint or rick-rack, glue, scissors, a hole punch, and the gingerbread people **Reproducible** on page 44.

Give each student two squares of fine sandpaper and a copy of the Reproducible. Then guide your class through the following steps:

1 Cut out the gingerbread people on the Reproducible. Using a marker, trace a gingerbread figure on the back of each piece of sandpaper.

2 Glue your two gingerbread shapes together with the sandpaper sides facing out. Let the glue dry.

3 Slowly and gently rub your cinnamon stick across the sandpaper until the paper smells as sweet as cinnamon.

4 Decorate your gingerbread people with white fabric paint or rick-rack to look like frosting. Punch a hole in the top of your gingerbread person and thread it with string to make a hanging decoration.

Winter Cardinals

As you learn about the habits of winter birds, make and hang these colorful cardinals in your classroom window.

For each bird, you will need construction paper, tissue paper, markers, string or yarn, glue, hole puncher, scissors, a ruler, and the **Reproducible** on page 45.

Give each student a copy of the Reproducible and then guide the class through the following steps:

1. Trace the cardinal shape onto red construction paper and then cut it out.

2. Cut out the bird's head and glue it in place. Color the beak yellow or white.

3. Fan-fold a 2" length of tissue paper for a tail, stapling the "fan" at one end. Then glue the tissue paper tail to the bird.

4. Cut a 4" length of tissue paper to make the wings and fan-fold it lengthwise.

5. Cut a slit in the bird as shown, and insert the tissue paper half way. Fold it open on each side and glue the inner edges against the body.

6. Punch a hole high on the bird's back and thread a piece of string or yarn through it.

Super Snow Globes

Capture the season and enhance your winter study units with paper snow globes.

For each snow globe, you will need construction paper, markers, plain white paper, scissors, hole puncher, glue, and the **Reproducible** on page 45. Give each child a copy of the snow globe Reproducible and then guide your class through the following steps:

1. Trace the globe pattern onto blue construction paper and cut it out, then trace the base pattern onto brown construction paper. Glue the globe onto the base.

2. Using markers and scraps of paper, create a winter scene, such as a snowman in a forest, to place inside the globe. Add snow by glueing on white dots made with a hole puncher.

3. Cover the globe with plastic wrap, taping the wrap securely to the back.

—*Barb Roberts, Walberta Park School, Syracuse, NY*

Use with **Cool Cookie Jars**, page 42.

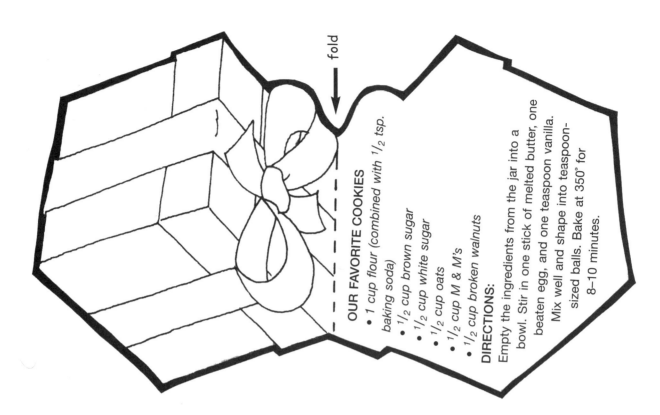

fold

OUR FAVORITE COOKIES
• 1 cup flour (combined with 1/2 tsp. baking soda)
• 1/2 cup brown sugar
• 1/2 cup white sugar
• 1/2 cup oats
• 1/2 cup M & M's
• 1/2 cup broken walnuts

DIRECTIONS:
Empty the ingredients from the jar into a bowl. Stir in one stick of melted butter, one beaten egg, and one teaspoon vanilla. Mix well and shape into teaspoon-sized balls. Bake at 350° for 8–10 minutes.

Use with **Gingerbread People**, page 43.

Use with **Winter Cardinals**, page 43.

Use with **Super Snow Globes**, page 43.

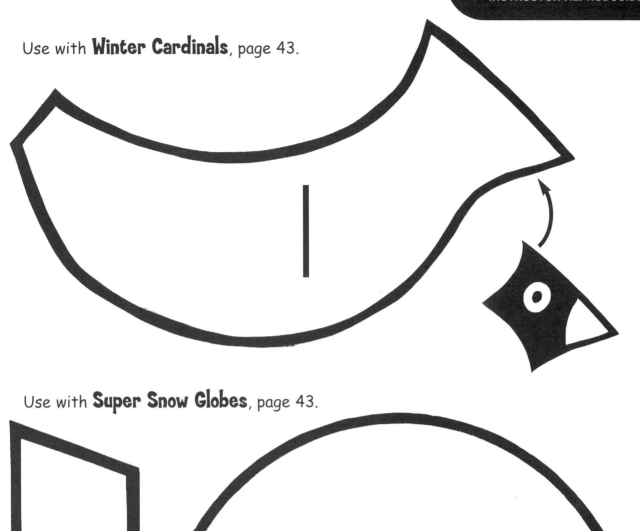

Storybook 100 DAYS

Activities for the book *Emily's First 100 Days of School*
By Jacqueline Clarke

Read Rosemary Wells's book *Emily's First 100 Days of School* (Scholastic, 2000) with your students and join Emily as she counts up the days until the hundredth day of school. Along the way, Emily examines each "number friend" as it relates to something in her world—24 cookies for open house, 32 Girl Scout merit badges, and 50 stars on the U.S. flag. Extend the book with these activities that explore not only 100, but also the numbers 1–99.

Number Scavenger Hunt
Emily saw 3 on her bus, 35 on a stamp, and 42 on a street sign. Conduct a scavenger hunt in which students will learn, like Emily, how numbers are used in everyday life.

Give each child a hundreds board and conduct a field trip within the school and in the surrounding neighborhood. Challenge children to search for numbers 1–100, and have them cross off the numbers as they find them. When students bring their boards back to school, invite them to draw and write about a few examples of the places where they found numbers (e.g., on a street sign, in the cafeteria, or in a local store). Display the examples on a bulletin board, under the heading "Numbers in My World."

Top 100th Day Web Pick
Visit Education World's "Celebrate the 100th Day in 100 Ways" for more great ideas to use in your classroom!
www.education-world.com/a_lesson/lesson149.shtml ■

Number Facts Book
Woven into *Emily's First 100 Days of School* are number facts such as "there are nine planets in our solar system." Work together with students to create a collaborative fact book about numbers, based on information discovered during units of study. To make the book, gather 25 sheets of paper. Draw a line across each page (both sides), creating four boxes per sheet of paper. Number the boxes 1–100. Add a decorative cover. Punch holes on the left side and bind together, using yarn. Work together with students to add facts to the book as you encounter them in your curriculum. Challenge students to find facts for all the numbers 1–100 by the end of the school year.

100th Day Letters
On the 100th day, Emily writes a letter to her family telling them what she has learned to do since the first day of school. She signs her letter with 100 kisses. Invite students to write similar letters to their own families. In turn, write a letter to students highlighting the things you have learned in the past 100 days. Thank them with 100 chocolate kisses in a zip-top bag that has been attached to the letter. Ask students, "If we divide the kisses evenly among the class, how many will each child get?"

100 Wish List
On day 100, Miss Cribbage says, "I can think of a hundred new things to do!" Work together with students to create a wish list of 100 things they would like to do before the end of the school year. Explain that each idea should be something that includes everyone, can be done at school (or in the classroom), is safe, and costs no money. For example, play bingo, eat lunch in the classroom, read a current favorite book, and so forth. Write each idea on a slip of paper and place the slips in a box or bag. For the rest of the school year, reward the class for good behavior by choosing an idea and completing the activity.

Name _____

Hip Hip Hooray for the 100th DAY!

Directions:

1. Find each number pair on the graph. Make a dot for each.

2. Connect the dots in the order that you make them.

3. What picture did you make? _____

Across	2	3	4	5	6	7	8	9	7	4	2
Up	9	6	3	0	2	3	4	4	6	8	9

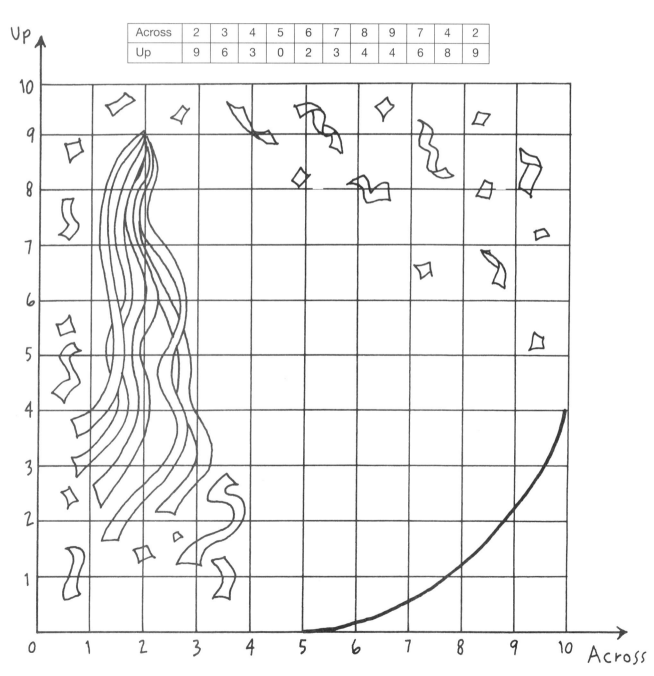

Life in the ARCTIC TUNDRA

Take students on an imaginary expedition to the frozen desert of the Arctic tundra

By Mackie Rhodes

Getting Started Set up a wintry reading display of tundra-themed books. Include laminated articles and photos from magazines such as *Science World* or *National Geographic Kids* and inspiring props such as a stuffed polar bear, furry earmuffs, mittens, ski goggles, maps, or a globe. Then introduce your unit with the Animals of the Arctic Tundra **Reproducible** on page 50. Invite students to record their questions and discoveries in "Arctic Field Journals," decorated with their own drawings of tundra animals. You can also create a KWL chart by having students add sticky notes to an Arctic map.

Bundled in Fur Many Arctic animals, such as musk oxen, wolves, and foxes, grow two layers of fur to help insulate them in subzero winter temperatures. The animals shed this extra layer each spring, when temperatures rise and the extra layer is no longer needed.
Activity: To demonstrate how extra fur benefits animals, fill the bottom of a cooler or tank with ice. Invite students to take turns putting on a pair of cotton garden gloves, which represent a single coat of fur. On one hand, slide a large leather glove over the cotton glove to represent an animal's additional coat of fur. Then have the student hold both hands above the ice for a minute or two. Which hand stays the warmest? Why? Give each student a chance to try this experiment.

Camouflage Coats Many tundra animals (such as foxes, hares, wolves, and polar bears) and tundra birds (such as snowy owls and terns) grow white outer fur or white feathers to help camouflage them on the snow-covered winter landscape.
Activity: To help students understand how camouflage works, add a tundra ecosystem model to your Arctic reading center. Fill up a plastic swimming pool with white quilt batting and crumpled white tissue paper. Or have students brainstorm other materials that they can arrange to resemble the snowy tundra. Then invite them to add photographs, drawings, clay models, and stuffed versions of some of the tundra's permanent animal and bird residents. Once these are all in place, ask students to step back to view the tundra scene they've created. Does the snowy landscape help or hinder their ability to spot the creatures? Why?

Wolf Packs and Fox Kits

Arctic wolves and Arctic foxes share many traits. Both live in groups (either *packs* or *kits*), and have an important part to play in the arctic ecosystem. But wolves are much larger and hunt large mammals, such as caribou.
Activity: Invite your class to form two teams, the Arctic Wolves and the Arctic Foxes. Encourage them to find out how their chosen animal lives and survives. What are its habits, life cycle, and adaptations to the harsh cold? What is the sound of its call? Then as each team presents their new knowledge to the class, have students create Venn diagrams (labeled "wolves," "foxes," and "both") with words or illustrations. Each team can use their diagrams to write a collaborative book on their animal, complete with a team logo.

Snowy Owl

Arctic Fox

Arctic Wolf

Arctic Tern

The Tundra Comes to Life

Some Arctic animals and birds have adapted to survive the harsh winters, while others live there only in the summer. These creatures arrive in spring to raise their young and eat the abundant food. In the winter, they migrate southward to warmer climates. Every tundra animal, bird, and plant plays a crucial role in a food chain.

Activity: Ask students to each pick an animal that lives on the tundra and research more about its life cycle. Ask students: When does your animal live on the tundra? How does it fit into an Arctic food chain? Then ask them to illustrate this chain on a large sheet of paper, with a speech bubble drawn beside each animal or plant. Inside the bubbles, have students write a sentence from each organism's perspective describing how the organism contributes to the chain of life. For example, in a chain of a poppy flower, an Arctic hare, and an Arctic fox, the hare's speech bubble could say, "I eat poppies. Sometimes I become food for foxes," while the fox's bubble could say, "I eat hares, lemmings, and fish. My waste fertilizes the tundra soil."

Growing at the Speed of Summer

Summer on the tundra is very short, so plants must make efficient use of the long daylight hours. They *photosynthesize* constantly, using energy from the sun to make food, which allows them to bloom at a fast rate.

Activity: Invite students to explore the effect of extended daylight on the growth of plants. Together with students, prepare two identical pots of soil, and plant the same kind of fast-growing seeds (such as grass or marigolds) in both. Place one pot in an area where the plant will be exposed to the natural pattern of daylight and night, and the other in an area where a fluorescent plant light (available at gardening stores) can shine on it 24 hours a day. Then have students observe and compare the plants daily. Ask: Did extended exposure to light speed the plant's growth rate? Why?

Willows in the (Arctic) Wind

Tundra willow trees grow to only about 6 feet tall and hug the ground to escape the fierce Arctic winds, which would topple taller trees. In the winter, snow blankets these little trees and protects them from sharp tundra ice crystals.

Activity: Invite students to create models to demonstrate the effect of wind on trees of different sizes. Have them twist two pipe cleaners together to create a tree trunk, leaving about 1" loose at one end to represent the roots. Have them attach and shape pipe-cleaner branches that extend in several directions. Then ask students to shape another pair of pipe cleaners into a tiny, short tree with long, low limbs and roots. "Plant" both trees in a mound of clay "soil" and press firmly onto a tabletop. Ask students to blow on the trees as hard as they can. How do the two trees respond? What happens when tall trees are exposed to strong, sustained wind?

Shallow Roots in the Soil

Only the top few inches of tundra soil thaw in the summer because the ground beneath it is *permafrost*. Since roots can't penetrate or thrive in frozen soil, they grow horizontally instead of vertically. This is another reason why tundra trees are short—shallow roots don't anchor tall trees very well!

Activity: Invite students to try growing their own plants with shallow roots. Have small groups of students each put an inch of soil in a clear container and add fast-growing seeds. As students care for the plants, ask them to observe how long the seedlings thrive in shallow soil, which way the roots grow, and whether or not the plants sprout.

ANIMALS of the ARCTIC TUNDRA

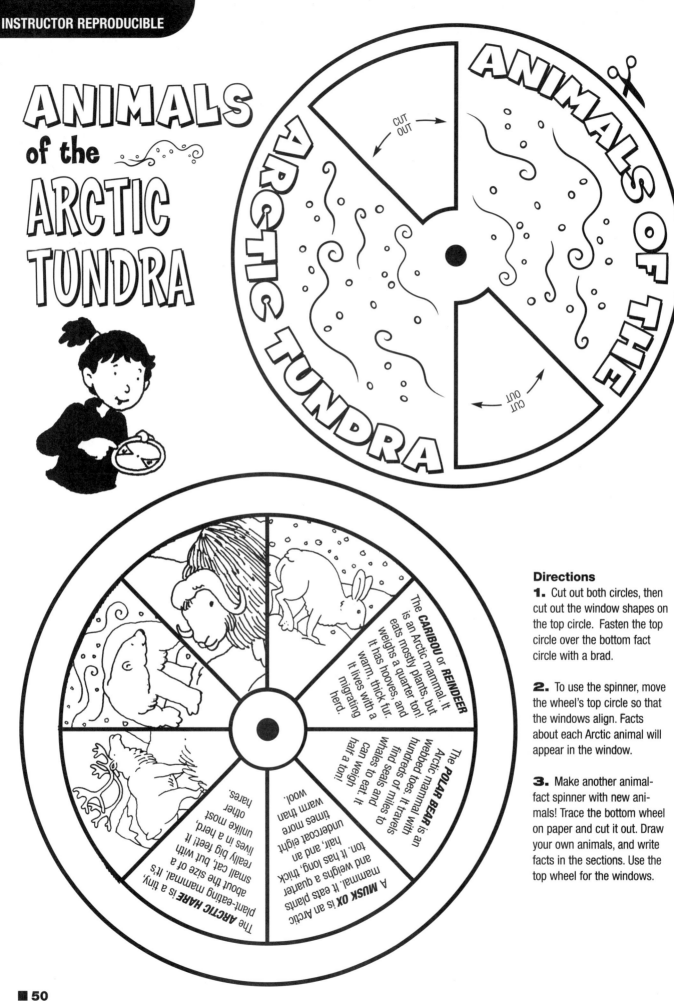

ANIMALS OF THE ARCTIC TUNDRA

CUT OUT →

← CUT OUT

The **CARIBOU** or **REINDEER** is an Arctic mammal. It eats mostly plants, but weighs a quarter ton! It has hooves, and warm, thick fur. It lives with a migrating herd.

The **POLAR BEAR** is an Arctic mammal with webbed toes. It travels hundreds of miles to find seals and whales to eat. It can weigh half a ton!

A **MUSK OX** is an Arctic mammal. It eats plants and weighs a quarter ton. It has long, thick hair, and an undercoat eight times more warm than wool.

The **ARCTIC HARE** is a tiny, plant-eating mammal. It's about the size of a small cat, but with really big feet! It lives in a herd, unlike most other hares.

Directions

1. Cut out both circles, then cut out the window shapes on the top circle. Fasten the top circle over the bottom fact circle with a brad.

2. To use the spinner, move the wheel's top circle so that the windows align. Facts about each Arctic animal will appear in the window.

3. Make another animal-fact spinner with new animals! Trace the bottom wheel on paper and cut it out. Draw your own animals, and write facts in the sections. Use the top wheel for the windows.

IF I WERE PRESIDENT...

Usher your students into the Oval Office with our patriotic Presidents' Day activities. Plus! A bonus White House Reproducible **By Mackie Rhodes**

Presidential Poster Gallery

Creating a gallery of presidential profiles is a great way to begin learning about the presidency. Provide research-starters for your students such as *Our Country's Presidents*, by Ann Bausam, and *Scholastic Encyclopedia of the Presidents*, by David Rubel. Have each student choose a President and research his life to learn important facts, such as birth date, home state, family members, work experience, accomplishments, and other interests. Then start your class on poster profiles of their Presidents, asking them to record highlights of their research information and add drawings and pictures. After the children share their posters with the class, display them around your room for inspiration and reference during your presidential unit.

Home State Map

Our Presidents have come from many different states from coast to coast. Assign each student to one or more of the 43 Presidents to research their home states. Then have children fill out slips of paper that read: I am _____, the _____ President of the U.S. My home state is _____. Display a large map of the United States and ask your students to find and mark all the home states with the slips of paper, attaching each slip to the appropriate state on the map. Extend this activity by having your child "presidents" write label slips for themselves and attach these new slips to their choice of states.

The Chief's Checklist

The President wears many hats and has many responsibilities. Write each title for the President (e.g. Head of State, Commander-in-Chief) on a paper hat cutout and glue the hats to a large piece of chart paper. As the children learn more, ask them to record on the chart

Paper Bag Flags • **What is Presidents' Day without flags and fanfare? Invite children to make these easy flags for this festive occasion. You will need one paper grocery bag with a handle for every two children. Have the children cut out the large panels of the grocery bag. They can use paint and craft materials to decorate the panel (handle to the left) to resemble an American flag or the presidential flag. Then invite students to wave their flags during the "Inauguration Day" activity. page 52.**

paper each new fact they learn about the president's job. Here are examples:
- The President signs new laws.
- The President gives a radio address each week.
- The President meets with leaders of other countries.

Chief Executive Ads

Now that your students have learned about the presidency, ask them to write classified ads for the position. Begin by sharing classified ads from the employment section of your newspaper. Then review the qualifications for the highest job in the land: The President must be at least 35 years old and a U.S.-born citizen who has lived in this country for at least 14 years. Along with these requirements, discuss and list other qualities that might be desired in a presidential candidate. Ideas might include professional skills such as the ability to budget money, lead the government, and command the military; and more personal traits, such as politeness and honesty. Afterward, you might also discuss the benefits of the presidency—good pay, a large home, planes, the opportunity to make a difference, lots to learn, and so on. Invite children to read their ads aloud. Who wants to apply?

Inauguration Day

Holding an Inauguration Day ceremony is a great way to help children understand the honor and importance of the ceremony. When the President is sworn into office on Inauguration Day, he makes an oath, or promise, to do his very best to serve and protect the nation. Read the president's oath to your class and show them the presidential seal—a symbol of the President's promise and responsibility. Then ask each child to write the promises that he or she would make to the nation as President. Have them fold their papers in thirds and decorate them with three-inch circles colored to resemble the presidential seal. Each student "president" should then recite the presidential oath and read his or her sealed promises.

Presidential Oath:
"I do solemnly swear that I will faithfully execute the office of President of the United States, and will, to the best of my ability, preserve, protect, and defend the Constitution of the United States."

Here Comes the Press!

With the title of President comes lots of attention, especially from the media. Appoint a "president" to stand in front of a group of reporters (students) equipped with pencils and paper. Display the chart from "The Chief's Checklist" for all to see. Have the reporters refer to the chart to construct questions to ask the president. When recognized by the president, have reporters preface their questions with "Mr. (or Ms.) President." After a specified time, ask the president to end the press conference, then send the reporters to their desks to write their press releases.

Web Sites:

- *The White House Site for Kids* www.whitehousekids.gov
- *The Presidents of the United States* www.whitehouse.gov/history/presidents
- *World Almanac for Kids* www.worldalmanacforkids.com/explore/presidents.html
- *U.S. Presidents Resource Tools* http://teacher.scholastic.com/research tools/articlearchives/uspres/index.htm ∎

My White House Guidebook • Each of your pretend
presidents has the imaginary privilege of living in the White House. At www.whitehousekids.gov, you can point out many of the famous rooms in this presidential home, such as the Oval Office, the Lincoln Bedroom, as well as the Red, Blue, Green, and Yellow Oval rooms. Have children research the history and use of these historically important rooms, then invite them to make their own White House book. In their books, students can illustrate a different White House room on each page and describe how the rooms would be used during their presidencies. To make the White House books:

1. Take eight sheets of 5" x 6" paper for each student, and staple the sheets along the left edge.

2. Give each child a copy of the White House Reproducible, opposite. Ask children to cut it out, following the thick black lines.

3. Ask each child to glue the cutout to a sheet of construction paper, inserting the stapled pages behind the flap, as shown below.

4. Give each student a sandwich-pick flag to tape on the White House roof!

Fun facts: Today's White House has 6 floors, 132 rooms, 35 bathrooms, 412 doors, 147 windows, 8 staircases, 3 elevators, and 12 chimneys.

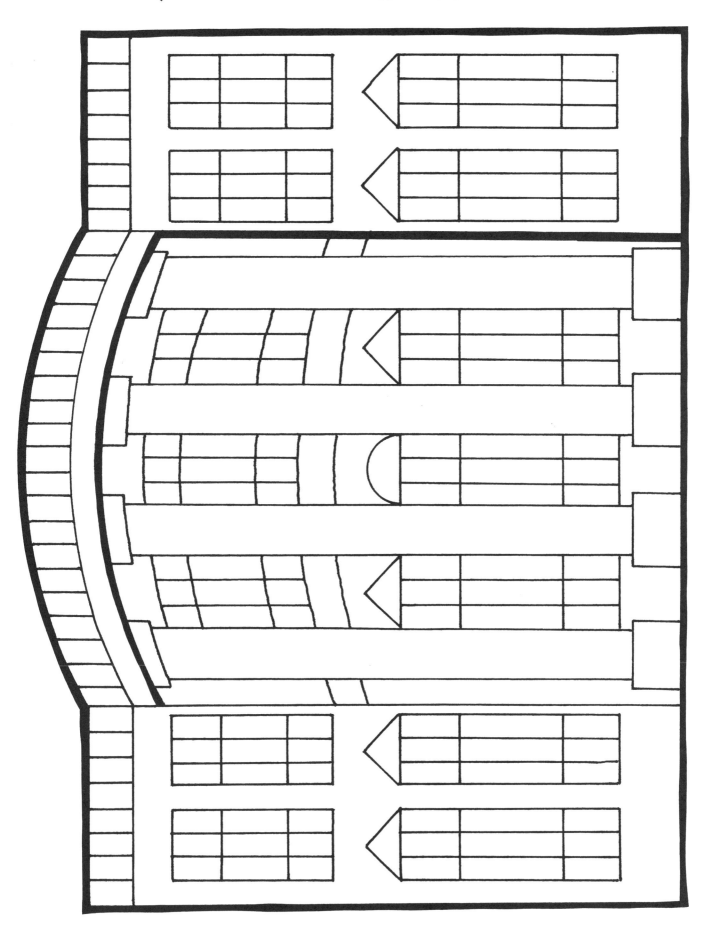

I HAVE A DREAM

An original play about
Dr. Martin Luther King, Jr.
By Mack Lewis

Sheltered by his loving family, young Martin Luther King, Jr. grew up happily unaware of racism—until a callous and prejudiced neighbor opened his eyes. This original **Reproducible** play (opposite) dramatizes a true episode from Dr. King's childhood and imagines how it might have started him on his lifelong crusade to end racism.

Before Reading

Talk about the context. Thankfully, most children have little concept of the legalized prejudice and discrimination that was common and accepted in the United States before Dr. King's time. Explain that for more than 100 years following the official end of slavery in 1863, there were, in effect, two societies—one for whites, and one, restricted and inferior, for blacks. Black people had to go to separate schools, sit in separate sections in movie theaters and on buses, and use separate drinking fountains. "Whites only" signs hung outside many restaurants and pools. This was the society Dr. King grew up in and the conditions that drove him to crusade for equality.

Talk about the genre. Explain that this play is a work of historical fiction: a story that is based on a true incident from history. The incident in the play is well-known, but the dialogue and some details are made up. Ask: What other works of historical fiction has the class read or seen? What other historical events would make interesting stories?

Assign roles. There are 10 characters in the play. Give more children a chance to read aloud by casting new children for each scene (25 roles in all).

After Reading

Scene 3: Why does Mrs. Conner make Mrs. King and Martin wait until the other customers are served? How might Martin have felt (angry, sad, confused, helpless, frustrated, etc.)?

Scene 6: Are Clark and Wallace prejudiced like their parents? (No, but they will likely learn from their parents' example.) Can we blame them for not playing with Martin? What do they lose because of their parents' prejudiced beliefs? (They lose a good friend and will perhaps lose more friends in the future. Their world becomes narrow.) ◼

Repro Script for Every Child
Pages 55–58

Directions: Cut out each page along the dotted lines.
Pile pages in order. Staple together to make a book.

I Have a Dream

SCRIPT BY MACK LEWIS
ILLUSTRATIONS BY EDUARDO ROSADO

CHARACTERS:

Narrator

Martin: Martin Luther King, Jr. as a boy

Clark and Wallace: The sons of the local grocer

Daddy King: Martin's father

Mrs. King: Martin's mother

Viola and Lorraine: Older women in Martin's church

Mrs. Conner: The grocer's wife

Adult Martin: Dr. Martin Luther King, Jr. as an adult

PAGE 1

Scene 1
THE SANDLOT

Narrator: Martin Luther King, Jr. grew up in Georgia back in the days when Babe Ruth was still hitting homeruns and movies were always filmed in black and white.

Clark: Pitch it, Wallace.

Martin: Can I play, too?

Narrator: Martin loved to play baseball with two white boys in the neighborhood.

Wallace: Martin is on my team!

Clark: I get him. He played on your team last time.

Wallace: So? I called it!

Clark: Don't try to push me around, Wallace.

Narrator: The boys would argue about who got to have Martin or his team. But even as a young boy, Martin was a peacemaker.

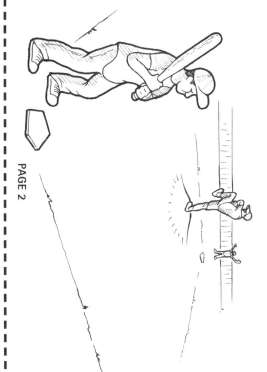

PAGE 2

55

Martin: No sirs! My daddy says you shouldn't fight like that! I was on your team last time, Wallace. I'll play for Clark today. That's fair.

Scene 2
THE EBENEZER BAPTIST CHURCH

Narrator: Martin's father was pastor of the church. They called him Daddy King.

Daddy King: Just as the Good Book says, we must love our neighbors as ourselves—whether black or white, whether young or old.

Viola: Look Lorraine, there's young Martin.

Lorraine: Martin, doesn't it make you proud to see your father standing so tall before the congregation?

Viola: Someday you're going to follow in his footsteps, Martin.

Martin: No, ma'am. I'm proud of my daddy, but my dream is to be a shortstop.

Narrator: Martin didn't know, but Lorraine and Viola were right about him. Someday he'd be known as the Reverend Martin Luther King, just like his father. But there would be some hard lessons along the way.

PAGE 3

Scene 3
THE NEIGHBORHOOD GROCERY STORE

Narrator: Clark and Wallace's parents owned a market across from Martin's house.

Martin thought it strange that whenever he and his mother went to the market, they entered through the back door.

Mrs. King: Excuse me, Mrs. Conner. I'd like two quarts of milk.

Mrs. Conner: You're going to have to wait. There are other customers in front of you.

Narrator: Like all black customers, sometimes the Kings had to wait to be served. Even when they did get served, they weren't always treated very well.

Mrs. Conner: Now, what is it you want?

Mrs. King: Two quarts milk.

Mrs. Conner: You'll have to pay before I get it. Do you have your money?

Mrs. King: Come now, Mrs. Conner. Have I ever not had my money? We both know it has nothing to do with whether or not I can afford it.

Mrs. Conner: It's just that I can never trust

PAGE 4

■ 56

Directions: Cut out each page along the dotted lines.
Pile pages in order. Staple together to make a book.

your kind.

Mrs. King: Our kind!

Martin: Your boy Clark is quite a ball player, Mrs. Conner. The other day he struck me out two times.

Mrs. Conner: You've been playing ball with my boys?

Martin: Yes, ma'am. They're my best friends!

Mrs. Conner: They are, are they? Here's your milk, Mrs. King. Head out the back.

Scene 4
THE CONNER HOUSE

Narrator: The next time Martin went to the sandlot to play, no one was there. He ran to the grocer's house and knocked on the door.

Martin: Where are your boys, Mrs. Conner? They were supposed to play ball today.

Mrs. Conner: Clark and Wallace can't play. They're . . . they're sick in bed.

Narrator: Martin could see past Mrs. Conner into the house. Clark and Wallace were standing in the shadows. Both boys were frowning, but Martin saw Clark shyly wave.

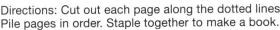

PAGE 5

Martin: Why, no they're not, Mrs. Conner. They're right there. Are you guys playing ball today?

Mrs. Conner: They can't play with you anymore. They're getting too old to be wasting time on coloreds.

Narrator: "Colored" was a word used to describe people whose skin wasn't white.

Mrs. Conner: Now don't be knocking on my door anymore.

Scene 5
THE KING HOUSE

Mrs. King: Why are you crying, Martin?

Martin: Mrs. Conner says that her boys can't play ball with me anymore. She says it's because I'm colored.

Mrs. King: I'm sorry. It was bound to happen sooner or later.

Martin: But why does my skin color matter?

Mrs. King: Some folks don't like people who are different.

Martin: But Clark and Wallace don't feel that way. We have fun together.

Mrs. King: The boys may not feel that way, Martin, but their parents do. That's why they make us use the back door. That's why they give us sour milk. They're punishing us for being different. And they'll teach their children to do the same.

Martin: But that's not fair. How can they do that?

PAGE 6

Mrs. King: There are laws that allow them to discriminate against us.

Narrator: Mrs. King was talking about Jim Crow laws. These laws made it legal for white people to treat black people unfairly.

Martin: Well, somebody needs to do something about it.

Mrs. King: Yes, Martin. Somebody does.

Scene 6
THE SANDLOT

Narrator: Someday Martin would do something about Jim Crow laws. But back when he was a boy, he just wanted to play ball.

Clark: Hey look, it's Martin!

Wallace: Don't talk to him. Remember what Pa said.

Clark: Sorry, Martin. We could use a shortstop, but our pa says he'll whip us if we play with you.

Martin: But what do you think? How come my skin color didn't matter last week?

Wallace: We don't want any trouble, Martin. We just do what we're told.

Scene 7
WASHINGTON, D.C.

Narrator: Years after Martin was told he couldn't play ball, he would preach to more than 200,000 people of every race and color in Washington, D.C.

Adult Martin: I have a dream that this nation will one day . . . live out the true meaning of its creed: "We hold these truths to be self-evident, that all men are created equal."

Narrator: Over the years Martin would be arrested many times for standing up for himself. He would be beaten, stabbed, and spit upon.

Adult Martin: This will be a day when all God's children will be able to sing with new meaning, "let freedom ring."

Narrator: Yet through it all, Martin would follow his father's advice to strive for peace and harmony among all people. That's why we celebrate his birthday each January.

Adult Martin: When we allow freedom to ring . . . we will be able to speed up that day when all of God's children . . . will be able to join hands and sing . . . "Free at last, Free at last, Great God Almighty, we're free at last!"

The End

WHAT MAKES A SENTENCE?

Strengthen students' writing skills with 10-minute mini-lessons

By Cheryl M. Sigmon and Sylvia M. Ford

Sentences Are Complete Thoughts

Teach your beginning writers that a sentence expresses a complete thought or idea. Let students pick any topic, then model writing sentences about the topic on the board or a chart. Include one or two incomplete sentences. For example: *There are eight crayons in the box. The crayons are brand new. The black crayon. All of the crayons have sharp points. And paper covers. We use crayons when we draw.* Explain that a sentence must contain a complete idea. Then identify and discuss the incomplete sentences in your example. Ask volunteers to underline the complete sentences with one color and incomplete sentences with another. Other students can add words to change incomplete sentences into complete ones.

Sentence Stop & Go

One of the first writing conventions children learn is that sentences begin with capital letters. When your students are familiar with this concept, try this activity. With STOP and GO signs in your hands, lead children in a march around the room. Tell them that, just like drivers in cars, they should pay attention to your traffic signs as you hold them up. Then explain to them that writers must read signs just like drivers do—that every sentence has a STOP and a GO sign. The GO sign is a capital letter, which tells us the sentence is starting; the end mark signals that the complete idea has been expressed. Show students a paragraph on a transparency or on chart paper and work on it together, asking volunteers to circle the capital letters in green and punctuation in red.

The Who & What of Sentences

Teach children about the basic ingredients of a sentence— "who" (the subject) and "what" (the verb)—by sharing a mystery with them. Show them the following paragraph on the board or on chart paper: *Hickory, dickory, dock. __ ran up the clock. The clock __ one. __ ran down. Hickory, dickory, dock.* Let children help you fill in the blanks. Explain that some of these sentences were missing subjects or verbs: we didn't know who ran or what the clock did at one. Then write a short paragraph of your own and let students decide if each sentence is complete, with both a "who" and a "what." For example: *We walked to the fire house yesterday. We songs on the way. At the station climbed on the fire truck. The firemen talked to us about their jobs.* Read each sentence aloud with students and discuss whether it has everything it needs to be complete. Ask students to add the missing ingredients and read the revised sentences aloud. To extend, compose a simple story on the board or a chart, leaving out some subjects and verbs. On tagboard or sentence strips, write many subjects and verbs for children to choose and tape in the spaces. As long as their choices are right, let them be silly!

Using the Reproducible Discuss with your class how writing comes alive with "sparkle words," or words that richly describe the details of a person, place, action, or thing. Ask them to think about, for example, the difference between the words *big* and *humungous*. Together, brainstorm describing words and list them on a chart labeled "Sparkle Words" (for example, *spicy, drowsy, foggy,* and *prickly*). Then have students complete the Cupid Capers **Reproducible** on page 60 by replacing the outlined "flat" words with sparkle words.

Name _____

Directions: Cover the outlined words in the story with "sparkle" words from the list below.

CUPID CAPERS

Cupid is in a hurry. He has many | nice |

Valentine letters to deliver. He | gets | onto

his | great | motorbike and heads toward the

school. Uh-oh, Cupid has lost his way. There

he goes over the | big | bridge and across

the river. Come back, Cupid!

_____

sweet	tiny	rushes	purple
leaps	stinky	fancy	rusty
shiny	giant	noisy	jumps
cool	races	flies	broad

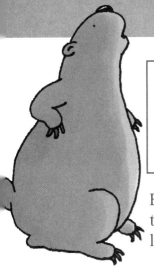

GROUND HOG AND OTHER COMPOUND WORDS

Each February 2nd, on Groundhog Day, we pay a visit to our furry friends to ask about the coming of spring. Extend the celebration by digging into a lesson on compound words with these fun-filled activities **By Mackie Rhodes**

Compound Word Whistle Use this role-playing game to help students identify compound words. First, ask children to search the room to find 10 compound words in print or to find items that are represented by compound words. Have them write each word on a separate note card and place the cards face up on their desks. Explain that when a groundhog senses danger, it whistles to warn others. In this game, children will whistle to let others know they found a compound word. To play, invite a "groundhog" to read a compound word from one of his or her cards. If any other groundhogs have that same word on their cards, they give a little whistle. Then all the groundhogs with the matching word turn that card face down on their desk. For each round, ask a different groundhog to read a word from his or her remaining face-up cards. Continue play until all groundhogs' cards have been turned face down.

Groundhog Weather Word Sort This activity is a fun way to boost students' categorization skills. To begin, brainstorm a list of weather-related compound words with students. Include

words that describe weather conditions (sunshine, thunderstorm), events (rainbow, snowdrift), and related items and clothing (snowmobile, raincoat). Then write the words on blank note cards. Place the cards in a basket and put them in a center. Also make a pair of groundhog-ear headbands and add these to the center. To use, two students don the headbands, pretending to be groundhog weather forecasters. Together they decide how to sort the word cards, such as by weather conditions or by common words. You might give students additional cards with suggested categories that they can use for sorting. When finished, ask children to describe their sorting rules and explain why any leftover words did not fit.

Using the Reproducible

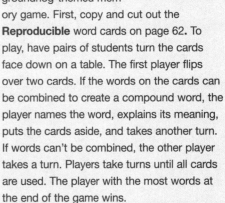

Send children on a compound word search with this groundhog-themed memory game. First, copy and cut out the **Reproducible** word cards on page 62. To play, have pairs of students turn the cards face down on a table. The first player flips over two cards. If the words on the cards can be combined to create a compound word, the player names the word, explains its meaning, puts the cards aside, and takes another turn. If words can't be combined, the other player takes a turn. Players take turns until all cards are used. The player with the most words at the end of the game wins.

Word-Building Relay Divide children into three groups for this challenging relay. First, give the class a topic, such as "on the road" or "lunchtime." Ask each group to brainstorm as many compound words as possible related to the topic. Then encourage them to look up their words in the dictionary to determine whether they are closed, open, or hyphenated compound words. Each group should then record their words in a three-column chart with the headings "Closed," "Open," and "Hyphenated." Finally, invite the groups to share their lists and add up the compound words that all the groups wrote.

Name _____

GROUND HOG A COMPOUND WORD GAME

Directions: Cut out each card below. Fill in blank cards provided with compound word parts (example: *ground* and *hog*). Follow your teacher's directions for play.

SPACE	FALL	TURTLE	ROAD	_____
BOW	ROW	SHIP	BOX	_____
KEEPER	KEY	LUNCH	EYE	_____
RAIL	TIME	HOME	NECK	_____
WORK	WATER	BOAT	RAIN	_____
SAND	LID	BOARD	GOAL	_____

Spring

Standards-Based Activities

Learning About Plants and Animals, Solving Word Problems,
Making Predictions, Reading for Meaning, and Much More!

SPRING ACTIVITIES From Our Readers

Crop Circle Geometry I motivate my sixth graders to learn geometry and measurement with a Mystery Crop Circles game. After they learn the formulas for determining diameter, radius, circumference, and area (which we display on large posters), I divide the class into teams of about four to five students each. Then we head outdoors! I set out different lengths of string, white and colored sidewalk chalk, and meter sticks. Each team, using string and some chalk as a compass, draws its circles on the sidewalk or blacktop. Then students race to correctly calculate the radius, diameter, circumference, and area of all of their team's circles. Later, teams get to customize their circles with extra designs and shapes to make them even more mysterious, and we take digital pictures to remember the learning fun. —Bonnie L. Noonan, Cedar Falls, IA

Pricey Patterns I make the required use of pattern blocks fun and interesting for my fourth graders with a Pricey Pattern Challenge. First, I assign a money value to each pattern block shape. Then I ask students to determine the value of a series of shapes. (For example, if the triangle is worth $1, how much is the parallelogram worth? The hexagon?) Once all the patterns have values, I have students plot these on a chart or graph. Then I invite students to create their own designs with the blocks and find the values using their chart as a guide. The possibilities for small group work or team games are endless: You can challenge students to create symmetrical designs, assign a value to each color, have teams race to calculate the value of the same design, and so on. —Mindy Messinger, Brooklyn, NY

My Multiplication Cards Your class will love these personalized, self-checking study cards! Invite students to choose and cut out favorite pictures from magazines, such as an animal or sports star. Next, have students glue the pictures onto construction paper. Show them how to trim their shapes so there is no more than 1" of paper around each image. To finish each card, punch holes all around the edge. Turn over and write the first half of a multiplication equation in the center and a different number next to each hole. On the front, write the correct answer next to each hole that corresponds with the number on the back. Students can check their sums by inserting their pencils in the holes. —Karen Pickett, Richmond, VA

Overhead Math Sentences
Leftover scraps of transparencies and laminating plastic can be recycled in so many ways. I cut the larger pieces into kid-size transparency sheets and store in a folder until needed. Then my second graders use the sheets to create math word problems with overhead markers. I put their transparency math sentences on the overhead projector and share with the class for whole-group learning and problem solving. My students beam proudly when their own transparencies are being shown to the class! Kids can also use the sheets to illustrate picture dictionary pages, the poems they've written, or life cycles of the different animals they've studied. —Linda M. Kuehn, Honeoye Falls, NY

Under A Rock

As spring approaches, I invite my second graders to go exploring outdoors with unusual nature "journals." To make these journals, students each need a sheet of lined paper and two sheets of construction paper: one a dark or vibrant color, and one a light shade of brown or green. Have students cut a rock shape out of the dark sheet of paper, then glue or staple this shape to the light-colored sheet along one edge to create a rock-shaped flap. Next, students cut a sheet of lined paper to fit on the inside flap of the "rock" and glue in place. Take students outside and encourage them to see how many different creatures they can discover nearby. Have them draw the bugs and critters on their journal pages under their rocks, as shown. Once back indoors, have students write a few sentences about what they observed. —*Diana M. LaRose, Bloomsdale, MO*

Place Value Shuffle

Here's a fun and easy way to reinforce place value skills. I give each of my fourth graders an index card with a single digit written on it, from 0 to 9. Then I call several students with their cards to come to the front of the room and challenge them to correctly arrange themselves as the largest or smallest possible number. When students are in place, I ask the rest of the class to call out the number, then decide if the arrangement is correct. I encourage all the students to have a turn out of their seats to participate. Later I vary this activity with team challenges to see which teams can create a specific number arrangement more quickly. We also use it to practice greater than/less than skills and to review place value column positions. —*Sue Petersen, DePere, WI*

Animal Word Problems

My first graders just love solving these hands-on word problems! I purchase a few inexpensive sets of small plastic animals with a specific backdrop, such as a farm or zoo, which students can decorate with additional hand-made fences, trees, and other props. I distribute a sheet with questions (or write questions on the board) such as: "How many cows were at the farm?" "How many pig legs did you count all together?" Then I invite students to come up and explore the animal display to get their answers. Later in the year, I ask more advanced questions, such as "How many more cows are there than pigs?"
—*AnnMarie Stephens, Manassas, VA*

Academy Awards 101

Each year after the Academy Awards in Hollywood, my third graders and I host our own! Each student receives an "Oscar" in a fun category. I use this activity as both a self-esteem builder and a unique language arts lesson. Students write out acceptance speeches to thank the important people in their lives. Then we invite families to a real ceremony where the kids read aloud their speeches!
—*Geraldine Batterberry, Sayville, NY*

★★ BEST SUPPORTING SPELLER ★★

★★ OUTSTANDING BEHAVIOR ★★
(IN A CLASSROOM ROLE)

★★ BEST SET DESIGN (ART) ★★

★★ BEST LEADING ATTITUDE ★★

★★ BEST DIRECTOR (READING) ★★

★★ MATH ACTION STAR ★★

★★ FILM HISTORIAN AWARD ★★
(ACHIEVEMENT IN SOCIAL STUDIES)

★★ BEST ORIGINAL SCREENPLAY ★★
(CREATIVE WRITING)

Kilometer Walk

One thousand meters is difficult to imagine, so every year my fourth graders and I walk a tenth of that, or 100 meters. We start at the top of the hill behind the school. One student holds onto the end of a string. Then the rest of the class and I mark off 100 meters with the help of a trundle wheel. At each 10 meters we stop, and a student holds up a sign with "10 meters" written on it. The class can look back to see 10 groups of 10 meters. Then we guess how far one tenth of a kilometer would be if we started at another end of the school and walk 100 meters again to check out our predictions. This activity is a great way to keep the kids motivated and to visually fix some of the concepts of metric measurement in their minds.
—*Bonnie Ephraim, Monroe, CT*

Spring INTO SPRING

Creative learning crafts from egg-carton insects to scratch-and-sniff art and recycled trash robots **By Annabel Wildrick**

Build an Insect

Scuttle into spring with a study of insect anatomy! Although insects come in thousands of varieties, all share these basics: three body parts (head, thorax, and abdomen), six segmented legs, and exoskeletons. Now kids can build their own unique insects.

For materials, you'll need cardboard egg cartons, each cut into four, three-part pieces; pipe cleaners, cut in half (six pieces per child); glue; scissors; a variety of craft supplies such as tissue paper, glitter, sequins, and natural objects; and the **Reproducible** (opposite). Guide children though the following steps:

❶ Select, color, and cut out the head, thorax, abdomen, eyes, wings, legs, and antennae for your insect.

❷ Glue the body parts to the three-part egg carton segment. To make legs, poke pipe cleaners through the egg carton and bend to anchor. You can then glue the paper legs to the pipe cleaners.

❸ Embellish the insects with pincers, claws, or other extras. Encourage students to use their imaginations as they select craft supplies. For example, can they imagine an insect armored with paper clips? Or camouflaged with crushed green leaves and bright flowers?

Trash Robots

In this Earth Day activity, students use recyclable materials to create large-scale robots. First, have students brainstorm a list of "found" materials to collect and bring into school.

You'll need any/all of the following: cans, various plastic and glass containers (rinsed clean!), cardboard, used tin foil, cereal boxes, paper-towel tubes, glue, tape, wire, and other useful "connective" materials. Have small, collaborative sculpting groups discuss the process by which they will construct the robots. Tell students that their robots must be at least as high as the shoulders of the tallest group member. Encourage artists to animate their robots by giving them active poses, then display the finished products in hallways.

Scratch-and-Sniff Art

In this activity, students create art that goes beyond the visual to incorporate the senses of touch and smell.

For materials, you'll need several pieces of corrugated cardboard (one per group), paint, sand, sugared drink mixes, glue, and materials such as cotton balls, beans, pasta, and feathers.

Take a walk outside and invite students to silently listen, look, sniff, and touch. Return to the classroom and ask students to share sensory words describing their experiences. Record these on the board. Next, divide the class into groups and give each a piece of cardboard. Guide groups through the following steps to make their art:

1. Draw a spring scene inspired by the sensory details you experienced during your walk.

2. To add three-dimensionality to your drawings, glue cotton balls, beans, pasta, and other tactile items to the cardboard.

3. Mix sand with paint, then use it to add color and a gritty texture.

4. For a sensory bonus, blend a sugary powdered drink mix with each paint color to make scratch-and-sniff flowers. When the works of art are complete, host an art show in which the guests are blindfolded and guided by volunteers.

scratch and sniff

Use with **Build an Insect**, opposite page.

Celebrate Dr. Seuss Day on March 2nd with activities inspired by his amazing books!   By Annabel Wildrick

Green Eggs and Ham

In a story about prejudging, Sam I Am tries to get his friend to eat green eggs and ham. Ask students to predict what a drink will taste like before they try it. You will need water, sugar, salt, lemon juice, orange juice, food coloring, plastic cups, straws, paper, and pencils. Mix one batch of each drink: clear (water and sugar), green (orange juice and blue coloring), red (salty water and red), blue (lemon juice, blue, and water), and orange (water and orange). Give students a straw, a paper with "Before" and "After" columns, and a pencil. Have

kids write down what they think each drink will taste like under "Before." Next, they can taste each drink and note it in the "After" column. Discuss the results. On what did they base their assumptions?

There's a Wocket in My Pocket

This silly little book is filled with great Seussian rhymes such as, "Did you ever have the feeling there's a zamp in the lamp?" Following Dr. Seuss's lead, students can create their own rhyming questions. To begin, pair kids up with each other or with adult guests. One

person asks, for example, "Did you ever have the feeling there's a kail in your _____?" The other person thinks of a rhyming word, such as "mail," to fill in the blank. The pair can switch roles to see how many rhymes they can make. Pairs can keep a list of their rhymes and share these with the rest of the class.

On Beyond Zebra

Young Conrad Cornelius O'Donald O'Dell learns from his friend that the alphabet continues after the letter *z!* There are many more zany letters, such as *wum, yuzz,* and *thnad.* Have students design and name their own letters, and then create words that begin with that letter. Ask them to imagine a creature or object that would fit this word. Keep art supplies on hand so that children may illustrate their words and write a sentence or two about their drawings. The letters can then be compiled into a class dictionary, which can provide a great resource for future creative writing projects. ■

Happy Birthday to You!   •   In this fun book, the Birthday Honk Honker leads
readers on an amazing trip through Katroo, where they really make birthdays special. Have kids make and decorate birthday-cake hats to wear for the day! **1)** You will need scissors, tag board, tape, yellow and orange pipe cleaners, yellow construction paper, glue, and markers. Cut out a cake top, 8" in diameter, with pencil-point holes punched through for the candles; the side of the cake from a sheet 26" x 4"; and 4 tabs, 2" x 1/2", bent into the letter *l.* **2)** Join the top and side of the cake together by taping the tabs to the inside of the hat. **3)** Cut the pipe cleaners into 3" pieces and twist the colors together. Cut flame tips from construction paper, and glue or tape them to the pipe cleaners to make candles. Push candles through the cake top and bend the ends to hold them in place. **4)** To adjust the hat size, cut two slits on the cake "band," overlap, and tape. Then, decorate!

Name _____

DR. SEUSS
Crossword Puzzle

Theodore Geisel, otherwise known as Dr. Seuss, wrote lots of books.
See how many you know by using the hints listed below!

Across
1. _____ on Pop
4. Bartholomew and the _____
5. Mr. Brown Can _____! Can You?
6. On Beyond _____
8. _____ the Turtle and Other Stories
10. The 500 _____ of Bartholomew Cubbins
12. One Fish Two Fish Red Fish _____ Fish
14. How the _____ Stole Christmas
15. If I _____ the Zoo
16. Fox in _____
18. _____ Eggs and Ham

Down
1. _____ for Diffendoofer Day!
2. There's a _____ in My Pocket!
3. The _____ Book
7. The _____ Battle Book
9. I Can Read With My _____ Shut!
11. Oh, the _____ You'll Go!
13. Horton _____ a Who
17. If I Ran the _____

TO BE... A BEE

Why do honeybees dance? How do bees carry pollen? Invite children to answer these questions and more as they explore the world of honeybees with these hands-on activities **By Mackie Rhodes**

Society in a Colony Buzz into your study of honeybees by helping children understand the roles within a bee colony. The *queen bee* lays up to 2,000 eggs per day to populate the hive. Thousands of *workers* attend the queen, nurse young bees, guard the colony, and supply food. *Drones* mature and mate with other queens. Draw a large hive on a sheet of brown bulletin board paper. Divide the hive into three sections and label them, from top to bottom, "Queen," "Drones," and "Workers." Then have children research and fill in the roles for each type of bee.

BEE FACT
Worker bees are female. They build the beehive and perform all the jobs necessary for the survival of the hive.

Busy as a Beehive

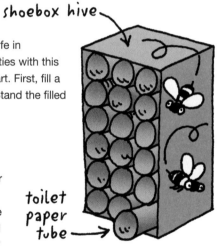

shoebox hive

toilet paper tube

With each individual bee dedicated to a specific job, life in a beehive runs very smoothly. Distribute classroom responsibilities with this easy-to-assemble job hive to encourage every child to take part. First, fill a shoebox with toilet-paper tubes, standing the tubes on end. Stand the filled box on its short end to create a tall hive. Paint with yellow tempera paint and let dry. Then insert into each cell a paper strip labeled with a classroom job. Have children help you create jobs based on the different roles of the bees and the way a hive operates. To use, children remove the paper from a cell and perform that specific job. At the end of the day, discuss how each child's efforts helped make the classroom a more organized and efficient "hive."

Pollination Observation

paint/pollen

A bee traps *pollen* on its hairy legs as it gathers *nectar* from a flower blossom. When it visits another flower, pollen falls off the bee's legs and *pollinates*—or fertilizes—that flower. This cross-pollination allows plants to reproduce. To demonstrate how bees transport pollen, have children make their own bees (see "Build a Bee," opposite) and cut out large flower shapes from construction paper. Sprinkle a thin coat of powdered paint in the center of the flowers, using a different color for each. Each paint color represents flower pollen. Invite children to gently land their bees on one flower center and then fly them to another. What happens as their bees move from flower to flower? Explain that real bees transport pollen in a similar fashion in order to cross-pollinate flowers.

Dancing Directions

When a bee discovers a field of nectar-producing flowers, it communicates its find by dancing on the hive. A circle dance means that the flowers are nearby. A waggle dance, in which the bee wags its abdomen, indicates the flowers are far away. To further direct the colony, the dancing bee waggles in a straight line, to the left, or to the right. Invite children to communicate in a bee's language. First, write the names of different classroom objects on note cards, making sure the objects are visible to students. To play, group children into "colonies." Then secretly show one "bee" in each group the note card. Instruct that bee to perform circle and waggle dances to give its colony clues to the location of the mystery object. When a colony guesses the object, invite the dancing bee to fly to the object to confirm its location.

BEE FACT
A beehive is built with wax produced in special glands in the workers' abdomens.

Build a Bee

The anatomy of a worker bee allows it to perform specialized jobs. Have students research a honeybee's anatomy and then build a bee with the **Reproducible** on page 73. First, children will cut out the pieces and tape each body part to black felt or construction paper and each wing to a folded sheet of waxed-paper. Then cut out following the patterns. Remove the patterns, paint yellow stripes on the abdomen, and glue the shapes onto a craft stick (as shown), trapping three 4" lengths of black pipe cleaner between the thorax and the craft stick. Next, glue two pipe-cleaner antennae to the top, a stirring-straw proboscis under the head, and a pipe-cleaner stinger at the end. Finally, glue on pom-pom eyes. Ask children to name the body parts and tell how each helps a bee perform its jobs.

BEE FACT
A bee has five eyes: two large compound eyes on each side of its head and three smaller eyes on top of its head.

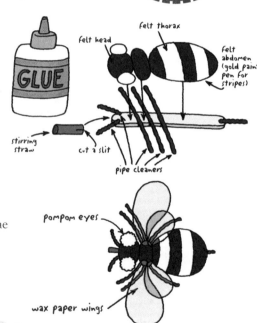

felt head • felt thorax • felt abdomen (gold paint pen for stripes) • stirring straw • cut a slit • pipe cleaners • pompom eyes • wax paper wings

Siblings by Scent

Explain to children that honeybees of the same colony recognize their siblings by scent. When an unrelated bee tries to enter the hive, guard bees detect its foreign scent and sting it to death. To help students understand how bees recognize one another, divide them into groups for this activity. First, gather a class supply of cotton swabs and three clear food flavorings, such as peppermint, coconut, and lemon. Divide the cotton swabs into three groups, dip each group into a different flavoring, and randomly arrange the swabs on waxed paper. Have children pick a cotton swab and form colonies (groups) by finding other "bees" with matching scented swabs. After the children have identified their "bee siblings," invite them to share their experiences.

How Much Honey?

On a single flight, a honeybee can visit more than 1,000 flowers, drinking nectar with its *proboscis*, a tongue that resembles a drinking straw. When its "honey stomach"—which holds only one-eyedropper's worth of nectar—is full, the bee deposits the nectar into hive cells. Group children into "colonies" for this activity. For each colony, place an eyedropper and cup of water at one end of the room and a plastic medicine cup (marked with teaspoon and tablespoon increments) across the room. To play, children take turns transferring water across the room to the medicine cups—one drop at a time! As the "bees" deposit their "honey" into the "hives," a recorder keeps count of the drops needed to produce the amounts of water, from one teaspoon to two tablespoons. When finished, explain that the drop count for each measurement equals the number of bee flights taken to produce that amount of honey. Tell children that each bee produces about $\frac{1}{12}$ of a teaspoon of honey in its lifetime.

Bee Math

Each beehive cell is a six-sided shape called a *hexagon*. Invigorate your study of bees with the following beehive math activities related to the number six.

Beehive Hexagon Puzzle: Give children a copy of the beehive puzzle **Reproducible** on page 73. Have them follow the guidelines to complete the puzzle.

A Hive of Sixes: On strips of paper, write equations representing the factors of six in addition, subtraction, multiplication, and division, including the answer for each on the back. Using the hive described in "Busy as a Beehive," insert each equation into a cell and place in your math center. To use, children choose a slip to solve from each cell. They can check their work by comparing their answers to the back of each strip. Challenge students to solve the whole hive! ■

Beehive Puzzle Answers

The Latest "Buzz" on Books and Web Sites

THE HONEY MAKERS

By Gail Gibbons (HarperTrophy, 2000). Covers the physical structure of honeybees, as well as how they produce honey and are managed by beekeepers. With beekeeper's journal and fact list.

BUSY BUZZY BEE

By Karen Wallace (DK, 1999). Filled with photographs, this book focuses on bee behavior and habits. With picture word list.

THE MAGIC SCHOOL BUS: INSIDE A BEEHIVE

By Joanna Cole (Scholastic, 1998). When Ms. Frizzle takes her class on a field trip, her famous bus morphs into a hive. The children become bees, of course, and gather nectar and gain admittance into the inner world of a beehive. Also available on videocassette.

DANCES WITH BEES

At the companion Web site to the NOVA program, your students can learn about the dances bees do to communicate, and other aspects of life in the hive. With bee facts, photographs, and a guide to additional Web resources.
www.pbs.org/wgbh/nova/bees

Use with **Build a Bee,** page 71.

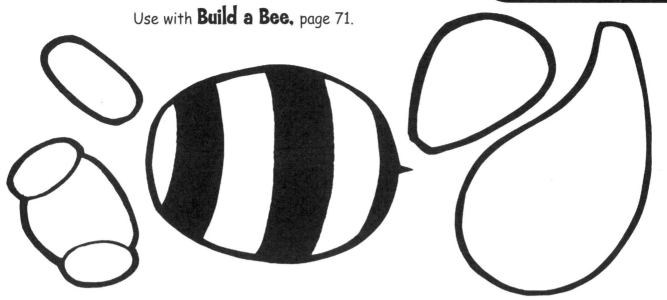

Beehive Hexagon Puzzle

Guidelines:
● Each number, from 1 through 6, should appear on each cell only one time.
● The sum of the numbers around each cell will equal 21.

Every Word Counts in HAIKU

By Liza Charlesworth

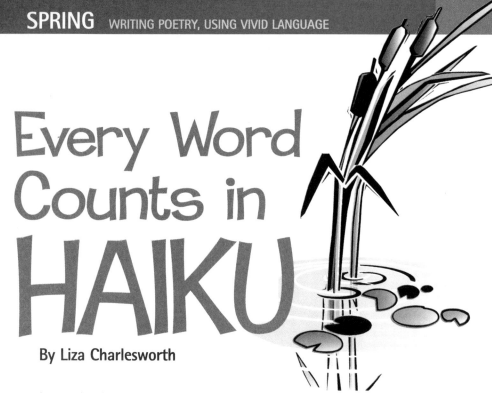

beautiful haiku—
like tender drops of nature
in a tiny box

A mere 17 syllables in length, haiku is one of the world's smallest works of art. But don't be misled by its miniature size. This deceptively simple verse is packed with emotional power and comes from a long history. Haiku, in its most ancient form, dates back to seventh-century Japan, where it was written—and chanted—to mark ocean voyages, praise emperors, and celebrate special harvest days.

Writing haiku is not as simple as it looks. It requires meticulous craftsmanship on the part of the poet—whether he or she is seven years old or 70!

Teaching Haiku

This poetry workshop includes two **Reproducible** pages: "Three Haiku" on page 75, and "How to Write Haiku" on page 76. Before sharing "Three Haiku," ask: "Is bigger always better?" Invite children to offer their opinions, guiding them to understand that beautiful things come in all shapes and sizes. Some are big, like a mountain or the Statue of Liberty, and some are quite small, like a four-leaf clover or a haiku.

Read the three poems aloud with the children, pausing to savor each gem-

like word. Ask kids: "What do these three works have in common?" Answer: They are each a "moving snapshot" of nature. It's as if each poet pointed a camera at a scene, then—click!—preserved that fleeting moment forever. Ask the children: "When you listen to the poems, what do you see in your mind?"

Separate the class into groups and ask each group to draw or act out one of the three haiku. What color are "translucent fishes?" How do you move like a firefly: "that way, this way, that way, this"?

Clap the Syllables

Bring the class together to play poetry detectives by clapping out each syllable—or beat—of Raizan's verse. You'll find its first line is five, its second line is seven, and its third line is five again. Does Issa's work follow the same pattern? (Yes.) What about Wakyu's? It almost does, but the second line is only six syllables. Explain that this poet used "artistic license" to break the rules, which enabled him to make his piece even stronger. After all, every word counts when it comes to haiku!

Listen to the Sounds

Mine these poems for examples of vivid verbs and apt adjectives. What language is the most memorable? Explain that *onomatopoeia* is when words sound like their meaning. Build elaboration skills by inventing a list of thoughtful replacements for "plunk-plash"—the sound a single frog makes when it jumps in the water. What sound does a diver make when he or she enters the water? A hippo? A house cat? Record the new versions on an overhead as you compose them together. Read your haiku chorally.

Writing Original Haiku

Get students warmed up to write their own haiku with an Itty Bitty Workout. Here's how: Give pairs of students three minutes to write teeny, unpolished poems on small items available in your classroom:
- a paper clip • a foil star
- a penny • a Lego

Invite volunteers to share their pieces to inspire classmates. Applaud all efforts—silly or serious!

After the creative juices are flowing, pass out the "How to Write Haiku" reproducible. Have children try to write haiku about a particular moment or feeling, rather than about an object. You can opt to have kids write in five-seven-five form or use an open syllable count. Challenge children to take their time, think deeply, and write a carefully-crafted haiku. Have kids recopy their poems onto gem-shaped cut-outs and publish them on a bulletin board entitled "Our Haiku Gems." ∎

THREE HAIKU

A giant firefly:
that way, this way, that way, this—
and it passes by
—Issa

There in the water
color of the water moves...
translucent fishes
—Raizan

Squads of frogs jumped in
when they heard the plunk-plash
of a single frog
—Wakyu

How to Write Haiku

There are different kinds of haiku. The most common is three lines long and contains exactly 17 syllables. The point of haiku is to capture one moment, one instant, one idea. So, for example, you wouldn't try to write a haiku about everything that happened to you in first grade or how much fun you had at the amusement park. But you might want to write about sitting in the front car on the roller coaster and heading over that first hill. It might read something like this:

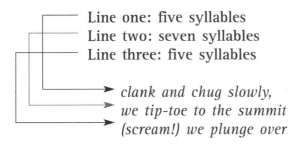

Line one: five syllables
Line two: seven syllables
Line three: five syllables

clank and chug slowly,
we tip-toe to the summit
(scream!) we plunge over

Now write a haiku of your own:

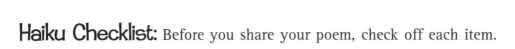

_____

_____

_____

Haiku Checklist: Before you share your poem, check off each item.

☐ I chose a great topic.   ☐ I edited my work.

☐ I used strong words.   ☐ I checked my spelling.

LEARNING ABOUT THE EQUATOR

Give a warm welcome to spring by inviting your students to study some of the hottest places on earth—the tropical rainforests, diverse cultures, and bustling cities along the 25,000 mile-long equator **By Linda Scher and Nathan Katzin**

Getting Started Did you know that the rainforests along the equator are home to more than half of the world's plant and animal species? Use this fascinating fact as a fun introduction to your unit. First, share several informational texts about the rainforest with your students, such as Kristin Joy Pratt's *A Walk Through the Rainforest* (Dawn, 1992). Then encourage students to learn more about one rainforest species that calls the equator home. Children can research their species in the library or online and then write a short paragraph about it. Finally, invite students to dress up like their plant or animal and share their research with the class. They will learn what a special environment the equator is!

Equator Map Hunt The equator anchors the latitude and longitude grid system that helps us find any place on a world map. Help students understand the function of this imaginary line using the Equator Map Hunt **Reproducible** on page 79, which challenges students to find several equatorial cities on a map. To extend, ask students whether each city is in the northern or southern hemisphere, and record their answers in a T-chart.

Countries of the Equator The equator passes through 13 countries: Ecuador, Colombia, Brazil, Sao Tome & Principe, Gabon, Congo, the Democratic Republic of the Congo, Uganda, Kenya, Somalia, Maldives, Indonesia, and Kiribati. Challenge your students to create a display about these unique and varied cultures. First, have teams of two students draw the name of an equatorial country from a grab bag. Then, give each team the **Reproducible** on page 78. Invite teams to complete an illustrated brochure that tells about the country they have chosen. The brochure should include the country's population, official language, average rainfall, and a picture of the country's flag. When finished, fasten the brochures together in the order above. The result is a super-sized display that takes the viewer on a journey along the equator step by step! ∎

Rainy Math Weather forecasting at the equator is a snap—most days the outlook is the same: warm with a very good chance of rain. Students will learn more about the equatorial climate and practice their predicting and research skills with this activity. First, have teams of two students

look up the average monthly precipitation in the capital city of an equatorial country. This information can be found online at www.weather.com. Then, based on these averages, encourage teams to predict how much precipitation will fall in one week. Students can check their predictions by recording the precipitation each day. At the end of the week students should add up their results and compare them to their original guesses. What accounts for the differences between their predictions and the amount of actual precipitation? As a class, graph all teams' results.

COUNTRIES OF THE EQUATOR

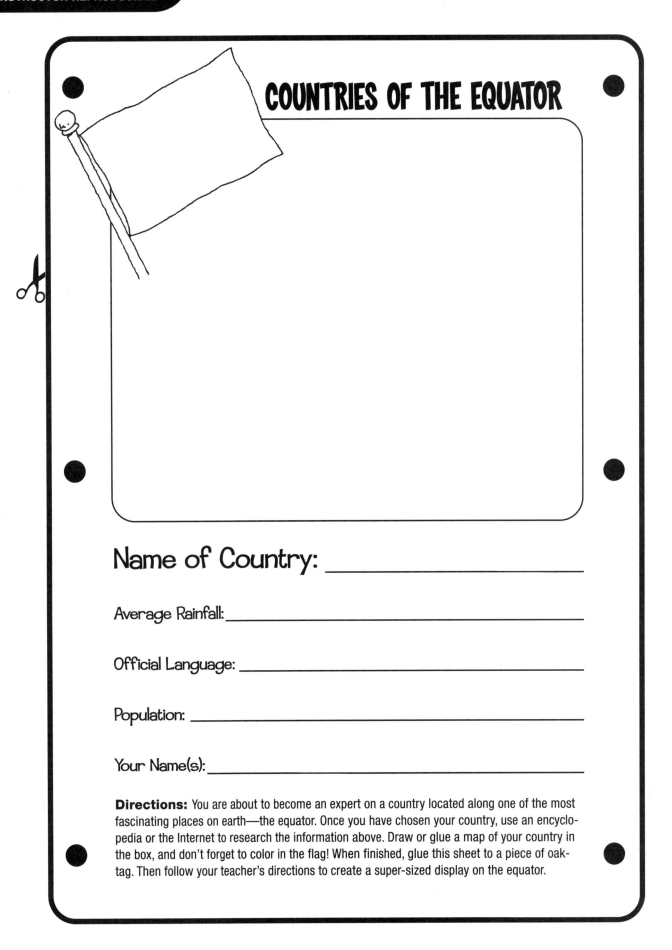

Name of Country: _____

Average Rainfall: _____

Official Language: _____

Population: _____

Your Name(s): _____

Directions: You are about to become an expert on a country located along one of the most fascinating places on earth—the equator. Once you have chosen your country, use an encyclopedia or the Internet to research the information above. Draw or glue a map of your country in the box, and don't forget to color in the flag! When finished, glue this sheet to a piece of oaktag. Then follow your teacher's directions to create a super-sized display on the equator.

Name _____

EQUATOR MAP HUNT

Directions: Solve the puzzle below by finding the cities and countries on the map where each pair of lines of longitude and latitude meet. Write the name of each city and country in the blanks next to its location. Then write the circled letters in order in the boxes.

LOCATION	NAME OF CITY AND COUNTRY
Longitude: 78 W Latitude: 0	_ _ _ ◯_ , E◯_ _ _ _ _ 　　　8　　　　5
Longitude: 32 E Latitude: 0	◯_ _ _ L _ , _ _ _ ◯_ A 　2　　　　　　　　　4
Longitude: 103 E Latitude: 1 N	◯_ _ P _ _ _ , _ _ _ G _ ◯_ _ 　3　　　　　　　　　　　　6
Longitude: 9 E Latitude: 0	_ _ B _ _ _ _ _ _ _ , _◯_ _ N 　　　　　　　　　　　　7
Longitude: 36 E Latitude: 1 S	N _ _ Ⓡ_ _ _ , _ _ _ _ A 　　　1

SOLVE THE PUZZLE

What mystery object should you bring with you on any trip to the equator? Write the circled letters in order in the boxes below to find out.

Ⓡ ◯ ◯ ◯ ◯ ◯ ◯ ◯
1　2　3　4　5　6　7　8

SPECIAL EDITION

Using newspapers in the classroom   By Mackie Rhodes

Extra! Extra! Learn all about it! Make headlines with these newsworthy cross-curricular ideas!

Daily Diagrams

What's the news of the day? Where's it happening? Who's reporting it? Review the elements of a newspaper article with students—the headline, byline, dateline, and body of the story. Then create a daily newspaper display to help students learn about the different parts of a newspaper. To prepare, cut out the title or flag of each section of your local newspaper—such as "World News," "The Nation," "Sports," "Lifestyles," "Arts," "Local News," etc.— and glue each one on a different colored sheet of large construction paper. Then laminate the sheets and display them on a bulletin board. Each day, have children take turns pretending to be the "editor" for each section. The day's editor chooses an appropriate article from his or her section, cuts it out, displays the article under its header, and highlights the headline, byline, and dateline.

Pass the Paper

Want a game that results in some quick-moving alphabet fun? Try Pass the Paper. To play, two or more teams of students are each given a newspaper and a sheet of chart paper. One child on each team begins by searching the newspaper for a word that begins with *a*. When the word is found, the child writes it on the chart paper, then passes the newspaper to the next team member. That child finds a word that starts with *b*, and records it under the first word. This continues until a team member cannot find the next word in the alphabetical sequence, or until a word for every letter has been found. The group that finds words for the most letters wins that round!

State Scavenger Hunt

Reinforce state names and locations with a newspaper scavenger hunt. To begin, provide groups of students with a copy of a newspaper and a map of the United States. Designate one child in each group to be the recorder. Then give a signal to start the hunt. To play, each group searches its newspaper for state names in the news. Whenever a state is found in print, the group highlights it in the paper while the recorder colors the location on the map. After a designated amount of time, figure out which group has found the most states. Or, wait until a team announces that they have found news articles about all 50 states!

Shopping Spree

Exercise students' consumer savvy with a shopping excursion through the daily newspaper. First, have children imagine they have a specific amount of spending money, such as $100. Tell them that they can use this money to purchase items advertised in the newspaper—as long as they don't go over the designated amount. To keep track, have kids create two-column charts, labeling one column "My Purchases" and the other "The Cost." After selecting two or more items, kids cut out and glue their "purchases" in the first column on the chart, using the second column to keep a running total of what they've spent. If they still have money left, students can make additional purchases, glueing in these items and adding the cost in the appropriate place on the chart. Finally, have children compare their charts to determine who came closest to spending the full amount.

Help Wanted

After discussing the organization and content of the help-wanted ads in your local newspaper, create a standard format for your own "classroom classified ads." For example, the format might specify that information appears in this order: job title, job description, candidate qualifications, job benefits, and contact information. Next have children name some classroom jobs that need to be filled, from weekly line leader to cleanup-crew member and calendar attendant. Using the format they've created, invite students to write ads for the job openings. Post these ads on a bulletin board near an office tray where kids can submit their job "applications." Written responses are sure to come pouring in!

It's Show Time!

Ask students to name some sources they might use to figure out when movies at a local theater will be playing. After discussing their ideas, distribute several newspaper ads that announce movie show times. Suggest that students create their own full-page movie ads based on the ads they see. To begin, have children imagine that a favorite book has just been made into a movie, and it is their job to create a newspaper ad for it. Within their ads, students should include a slogan for the movie and the times that the film will be shown. When they're done, students can swap papers and answer questions about their classmates' ads, such as, "How many times does this movie show daily?" "About how long is each screening?" and "If matinee screenings (before 3:00 p.m.) are discounted $1.00, how many opportunities do customers have each day to pay the lower price?"

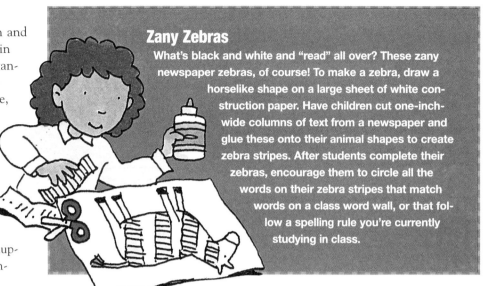

Zany Zebras

What's black and white and "read" all over? These zany newspaper zebras, of course! To make a zebra, draw a horselike shape on a large sheet of white construction paper. Have children cut one-inch-wide columns of text from a newspaper and glue these onto their animal shapes to create zebra stripes. After students complete their zebras, encourage them to circle all the words on their zebra stripes that match words on a class word wall, or that follow a spelling rule you're currently studying in class.

Comic-Strip Commentaries

Use a newspaper's comic pages to provide students with a little laughter—and a lot of writing opportunities! After examining several comic strips as a class, randomly distribute a different strip (one students have not yet seen) to each child. Have students glue each frame of their strip onto a separate large note card, numbering the front of these cards in the correct sequence. On the backs, have students describe the cartoon's setting, characters, actions, interactions, expressions, and dialogue in narrative form. Then have pairs of students exchange cards. The challenge: Figuring out the sequence of the strip they were given, based solely on the written descriptions by their classmates. Kids can then turn the cards over to check their work.

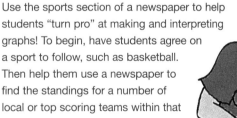

Go, Team, Go!

Use the sports section of a newspaper to help students "turn pro" at making and interpreting graphs! To begin, have students agree on a sport to follow, such as basketball. Then help them use a newspaper to find the standings for a number of local or top scoring teams within that sport. After students have taken turns transferring this data onto a master bar graph, hold a class discussion comparing the results. Track these same teams for a week or two, updating the chart as necessary. Then use the results to create a line graph showing how each team performed over a set amount of time.

Super Ball Challenge

Invite students to use the scientific method to design and build their own super balls! Begin by cutting open a baseball and showing students a cross-section of the cork core surrounded by rubber, woolen yarn, and leather. Provide similar materials (cork pieces, rubber bands, yarn, fabric) and alternatives like cotton and foil. Then have groups of students draw and label super-ball blueprints as they build their designs. Ask each group to specify in writing which materials it will use and why. Students can test their finished balls by dropping them from the top of a yardstick. Which designs bounced most? Least? Let students revise their theories and retest. How can they modify their designs?

Fast-Ball Physics

The faster a baseball travels, the more momentum it has. When a ball is caught, its *momentum* is transferred to the player's glove. For a visual lesson in this force, invite students outside for this experiment. Ask, "What do you think will happen if I throw a raw egg on the ground? Will it break?" Then toss an egg (enclosed in a sandwich bag); it will break because its momentum has been transferred abruptly. Next, have students hold up a bed sheet by the corners to make a net. Ask them to predict again what will happen when you throw an egg, then toss it as hard and fast as you can. Students will find that you cannot throw the egg with enough force to break it, because the sheet transfers the egg's momentum over a longer period of time, decreasing the impact on the shell.

PITCH-PERFECT BASEBALL SCIENCE

Get in the swing of spring with these activities of discovery By Sandra Markle

Baseball Freeze-Off

Baseball players have always known that the ball reacts differently on hot and cold days. Why do students think this is? Explain that a baseball is designed to compress and bounce back when struck with a bat. What do students think would happen if a batter were pitched an ice-cold baseball? A warm one? Which would work better? Invite students to share and then test their theories with this hands-on experiment. Give small groups of students each a yardstick and a room-temperature baseball. Have each group drop its ball a few times from the top of the stick and record the bounce heights. Next, chill the baseballs for at least an hour in a freezer or cooler of ice, then have students repeat the bounce tests. How accurate were students' predictions? Compile a line graph of the results on a bulletin board titled "The Great Baseball Freeze-Off," using baseball-shaped cutouts to mark students' graph points.

The Science of Baseball

The Sweet Spot Baseball players know that there is one part of any bat called *the sweet spot*. Striking the ball with this point of the bat makes the ball travel the furthest. Why do students think this is? Help them find the answer with this hands-on experiment. Give pairs of students each a wooden paint-stirring stick and a metal spoon. Have one partner loosely hold the stick while the other taps it gently with the spoon. The student with the stick will feel vibrations as it quivers. Talk with students about why they think this happens, then have them exchange roles. Next, choose a pair of students to demonstrate the same test for the class using a wooden bat and a hammer. As one taps down the length of the bat, ask your students to listen carefully; the sweet spot (about six inches from the fat end) will produce a different sound because it vibrates the least. Less vibration means more energy transferred to the ball. To extend this activity outdoors, let students dip a foam baseball in chalk and take a swing at it. The chalk will show how close each student came to hitting the sweet spot.

Batter Up! Some say hitting a baseball is the most difficult feat in sports. A batter needs quick reflexes and great hand-eye coordination. Invite students to test their own reflexes with this fun experiment. Stretch masking tape down the length of a plastic bat, then mark the tape into inches. Have partners stand facing each other, with one holding a bat chest-high by the handle and the other getting ready to catch the bat in midair. Have the first student (the pitcher) choose when to let go of the bat and the second (the batter) try to close his or her hand as quickly as possible to catch it. Have partners record the number closest to the batter's thumb, then switch roles. After repeating the tests, discuss whether practice helped students' reaction time. Later, the class can display its data on a bat-shaped graph.

Share these facts from Bouncing Science, *by Jess Brallier (Scholastic, 2002).*

● Baseball is great for teaching *physics*, the science of energy and how things move.
● Every action (like a bat hitting a ball) requires *energy*, the power that enables an action.
● When a baseball is struck, it compresses. As the ball returns to its original shape, it pushes away from the bat. This rebound is a *bounce*.
● *Weight* is the measurement of gravity's pull. More gravity pulls on an eight-pound bowling ball than on a five-ounce baseball.
● *Mass* is how much material the baseball contains. A ball has more momentum the more mass it has.
● *Momentum* is the strength of a ball's motion. It factors *mass* plus speed.
● *Impulse* is the force exerted on a baseball plus the time it takes for that force to be applied. ■

BASEBALL SCIENCE RESOURCES
BOOKS:
● *Sports Science Projects,* by Madeline Goodstein (Enslow, 1999).
● *The Magic School Bus Plays Ball: A Book About Forces,* by Joanna Cole and Nancy Krulik (Scholastic, 1998).
WEB SITES:
● Learning From Baseball
www.teachersfirst.com/baseball.htm
● Baseball Physics Glossary
http://library.thinkquest.org/11902 /cgi-bin/allterms.html

Sandra Markle is an award-winning author of more than five dozen books on science topics for children.

A Field Day for MATH

Add some bounce and zing into your math lessons with these fast-moving playground games **By Susan Dillon**

Hop-Skip-Jump Addition This relay race gets children moving—and adding like mad! Have two or more even-numbered teams line up in a row about 25 feet away from a pylon. Call out the first command: "Hop by 2s!" The first players in line must hop to the pylon and back, counting by 2s with each hop (2, 4, 6, 8, and so on). At any time, call out another command, such as "skip by 3s," or "jump by 5s." (Other commands to try: tiptoe, crawl, march, jog, sidestep, ice skate, swim.) The players start from zero with each new command. The players should round the pylon and return to tag the next player in line. This player continues where the first left off. When finished, the winning team jumps for joy—by 10s!

Beanbag Multiplication Try this toss-and-solve game to build early multiplication skills. First, draw a large chalk grid on the blacktop or sidewalk. Mark the numbers 1 through 5 along the top and down the left side. Provide beanbags, and invite children to step up and toss their bags at the grid. Wherever the bag lands, that's the equation they must solve. For example, if the bag lands on the axis point between 2 and 5, the child must multiply 2 x 5 and call out the solution. Challenge more advanced learners with a grid that goes all the way to 10. For more math fun, mark out a grid and ask students to each write an equation on a sticky note, then place one note inside each box. Invite children to step up, beanbags in hand, and try their luck!

Slam-Dunk Math Practice math facts and your hoop shots with this basketball game. (No hoop? Use any ball and a wastepaper basket.) Players stand in a line about 10 feet from the basket. A referee (you or another player) holds a pile of addition/subtraction facts flashcards and calls out the equations one at a time. For example, you call out "2 + 3!" The first player in line calculates the answer in her head, then bounces the ball 5 times as she walks toward the basket. When she stops, she calls out the answer and shoots. Then the next child takes a turn. For older kids, try using multiplication and division flashcards.

1 + 2, Touch Your Shoe!

In this rhyming game, players act out the solutions to simple equations. Kids can play independently or you can lead them in a group activity. For the youngest students and children with physical disabilities, make up and practice alternate movements together beforehand. Challenge older kids to make up their own verses!

1 + 1, reach for the sun
(reach up for the sun 2 times)
1 + 2, touch your shoe
(touch shoe 3 times)
1 + 3, touch your knee
(touch knee 4 times)
1 + 4, touch the floor
(touch floor 5 times)

1 + 5, take a drive
(make 6 turns of an imaginary wheel)
1 + 6, pick up sticks
(pick up 7 imaginary sticks)
1 + 7, fly to the heavens
(flap wings 8 times)
1 + 8, shut the gate
(shut gate 9 times)
1 + 9, chop down a pine
(axe chop 10 times)
1 + 10, do it all again!
(clap 11 times)

Summer

May–June

Standards-Based Activities

Learning About Other Cultures, Studying Ecosystems, Practicing Measurement, Predicting, and Much More!

SUMMER'S on the Way!

As days lengthen and brighten, celebrate by making super star piñatas, accordion journals, and venetian-blind paintings   By Annabel Wildrick

Cinco de Mayo Star Piñatas

Cinco de Mayo, the fifth of May, is celebrated as a national holiday by the Mexican people. It is observed with festivals, dances, and lively mariachi music. Students will enjoy making traditional Cinco de Mayo piñatas for a school party.

For each star piñata, you'll need a large balloon; papier-mâché (flour, warm water, newspaper strips); a large mixing bowl; twine; tissue paper; crepe paper; paint; glue; treats for the inside (candy, stickers, erasers); and the piñata faces **Reproducible** on page 87.

Guide groups through the following steps:
1. Color and cut out the reproducible faces.
2. Inflate and tie the balloon. Cover it with two layers of papier-mâché. Set it out to dry.
3. Cut a small, three-sided flap through which to remove the balloon. Fill the piñata with a selection of goodies. Close the flap and seal with another layer of papier-mâché.
4. Make six newspaper cones. Thread a 4' length of twine through the tip of one cone. (Tie a big knot on the end inside the cone.) Attach cones with papier-mâché strips.
5. Glue the happy/sad cutout faces to the piñata, one on each side. Decorate with tissue paper and paint. Attach crepe-paper streamers to the end of each cone. On the fifth of May, invite other classes to attend a party!

Accordion-Fold Journals

For a new twist on personal journals, teach kids how to make simple accordion-fold books in which they record their adventures, travels, dreams, and favorite summer stories.

For each double-sided, 10-page book you'll need two 6" squares of light cardboard, two 6" lengths of thin ribbon, nine 6" x 12" pieces of light-colored construction paper, glue, and scissors.

Guide students through the following steps to make their books:

❶ Fold each piece of construction paper in half.

❷ Using glue, overlap and join the pieces of paper with their folds facing in alternate directions.

❸ Glue one 6" square of cardboard onto each end piece, sandwiching a length of thin ribbon in between it and the page on each end. For variety, experiment with making accordion books out of different paper shapes, such as triangles, circles, and diamonds.

Venetian-blind Paintings

Invite students to create colorful "blinds" to decorate the classroom windows or walls.

For each painting, you'll need a sheet of colored construction paper, paint, black magic markers, scissors, and yarn.

Guide each student through the following steps:

1. Paint a colorful outdoor scene on a sheet of construction paper. Allow it to dry, then outline the images in black marker.
2. Cut the paper into several strips. Make sure that each panel is the same width. Cut two slits at the end of each panel.
3. Cut two long pieces of yarn.
4. Thread one piece of yarn through the first slit in the first panel. Knot it.
5. Thread the yarn through each slit in an over-under fashion. Leave a space between each panel. Knot and trim the yarn at the end. Repeat the process on the other side.

Use with **Cinco de Mayo Star Piñatas**, page 86.

Seashore Science

Wherever you live, your class can explore the sand and the sea with this "sun-sational" theme unit By Mackie Rhodes

Wade into science learning with our sand and sea activities. Start by making your own safe (and salty!) seawater. See the "recipe" in the circle on page 89.

The Salty Sea

Although oceans cover almost three-fourths of the earth and support an abundance of life forms, the water in the ocean is not fit for human consumption. To help the class discover why, give each student a small cup of seawater and a craft stick. Invite children to dip their craft sticks into the water and then taste it. What common flavor is in the water? Explain that seawater is unsuitable for drinking because of its high salt content.
Seashore Fact: Most of the salt in seawater is the same as common table salt. Too much salt intake can cause dehydration.

Water Weigh-In

Based on their first experiments, the children have discovered that seawater contains salt. But how does the salt content affect the weight of seawater? To find out, have children pour fresh water into one container and an equal amount of seawater into a separate, identical container. Ask them to weigh each container (or place the two containers on a balance). How do the weights compare?

Help the children make hypotheses and conclusions.
Seashore Fact: The salt in seawater makes it heavier, or more dense, than freshwater.

Dry Sand, Wet Sand

Waves are the primary means for sand to travel from the sea to shore and back out to sea again. Using only a clear plastic container filled with dry sand, help children discover how the sand and the sea interact.

1. Have the children tilt the tray back and forth. Observe what happens. Then add water until the sand is just damp enough to pack. Now tilt the tray. Unlike the dry sand, the wet sand remains in place. What happens when a seashell or the end of a straw is pressed into the sand?
Seashore Fact: Individual grains of dry sand do not stick together. But when sand is wet, water surrounds each grain and creates surface tension, which causes the grains to cling to each other. This is why it is possible to build a sandcastle.

2. Saturate the sand with more water until it becomes soft and mushy. Tilt the tray and observe what happens to the now saturated sand. Then have the children try to make a seashell impression in the sand. The sand will not hold the shape of the impression. Why?
Seashore Fact: When sand becomes saturated with water, the individual

grains separate so that the sand cannot be packed or even hold a shape.

Grain-by-Grain Erosion

Sand is a small particle of rock—a result of erosion over many years. Although tiny, grains of sand can also be the cause of erosion. To understand how, have children isolate a grain of sand and then rub it over a piece of foil with their fingertips. What happens? Explain that, just as the sand "cuts" into the surface of the foil, it can also cut into (or erode) the surfaces of surrounding structures.
Seashore Fact: Along the seashore, houses and docks can be eroded by the tiny, hard granules of sand that are washed or blown against them.

Seashore Sensory Surprises

Sand from the seashore is full of surprises. To help children discover this unique habitat, put items such as a starfish, a seahorse, or driftwood in separate pillowcases. Then have children take turns reaching into the pillowcase to feel each item. Ask them to write a description of the item and guess what it is. Then read the descriptions for each object, removing the object from the pillowcase. Afterwards, the children can add information to their descriptions based on their observations of the items.

Crystal Creations

Ocean water is replenished by the water cycle. But what happens to the salt in seawater during this process? Pose this question to students. Then provide them with sheets of foil, eyedroppers, and containers of seawater colored with food coloring. Invite children to use the droppers to make colorful designs on the foil. Set their creations in the sun to dry. As the water evaporates, salt crystals are left on the foil.

Seashore Fact: As saltwater evaporates, it leaves the salt behind. At the beach, salt residue can be seen on the surface of cars and windows, and even on skin.

Recipe for Seawater: Add 1/4 cup of salt for every 1 cup of hot water. Stir with a large wooden spoon, and then let the water cool.

Wave Explorations

Wave Explorations Floating objects on or beneath the sea's surface are moved about by waves. You can explore the science of waves using a large aquarium tank (or a long, clear plastic storage container, such as the 66-quart size). Use a wipe-off pen to mark inch-wide increments from top to bottom along the side of the tank. Place the tank on a sheet of plastic and fill it two-thirds full with water. Then mark the water line. Ask students to record their observations in a journal as they do the following experiments:

1. From one end of the tank, have the children blow air gently across the surface of the water. What happens? Repeat several times, asking them to blow with more force each time.

2. Float an empty film canister in the middle of the tank. Have children create gentle waves at one end. What happens to the canister?

3. Use a flat paddle to create waves at one end of the tank. With the water line as a reference point, record the height of each wave's crest (top) and the depth of its trough (dip). For each wave, the two should be about the same distance above/below the water line.

Seashore Fact: The speed of the wind usually determines the power of a wave: the more wind speed, the bigger the wave. Floating objects remain in almost the same place after a wave passes through.

Buoyancy Boat Ask students to speculate on whether or not the density of seawater will affect an object's buoyancy (its ability to float). Invite them to make a buoyancy boat to test their ideas. To make one, use a permanent marker to mark 1/8" increments along the side of a plastic applesauce cup or similar container. Then press play dough into the bottom of the cup, distributing it so that the cup sits level when placed in water. (Add a sandwich-pick flag, if you like.) First float the cup in a container of fresh water. Record the level of the water to see how much water is displaced by the boat. Repeat the procedure using seawater. Have students compare and discuss their observations.

Seashore Fact: The salt in the denser seawater pushes up against an object, making it more buoyant (able to float higher) than in fresh water.

Toothpick
Applesauce Cup
Playdough

From sandwich boards to story stew, celebrate a year of great classroom reads

Some of the most enjoyable teaching moments are those spent reading with children. Revisit your students' favorite stories as you close the book on another great school year!

Sandwich Board Book Parade

Celebrate and advertise your class's favorite books with sandwich board book signs. Each child or team will need two poster boards. On the front poster board, have the children recreate the cover or illustrate an important scene. On the back poster, ask them to write a short synopsis. Then, make the shoulder straps by stapling lengths of ribbon or string to the two poster boards. Hold a classroom or hallway parade so everyone can see what your class has been reading!
—*Bob McMeans, Corrigan-Camden Elementary School, Corrigan, TX*

Top Ten Countdown

Ask students to nominate and vote on their top 10 unforgettable books read during the year. Revisit one book per day as you count down the last 10 days of school. Invite school personnel such as the principal or guidance counselor to

reread the books to students during shared reading time. Students might also visit other classes to share their top 10 favorites.
—*Wendy Wise Borg, Maurice Hawk School, Princeton Junction, NJ*

Video Book Talks

Look out Reading Rainbow, here we come! Have each student prepare a talk based on his or her favorite book, and include the book's title, author, and a brief summary. Students can even end their talks with Reading Rainbow's classic sign-off, "But don't take my word for it, read ____ by ____ for yourself." Videotape each student performing a book talk and share the compilation with next year's class to introduce great books they'll encounter during the year.
—*Natalie Vaughan, Rancho Encinitas Academy, Encinitas, CA*

Story Stew

The ingredients from past read alouds are just the spice your students need to create enticing new stories. Provide small groups with a book that you read together over the past year. Have group members work together to record their book's characters, plot, and setting on separate slips of paper. Then have each group add their "ingredients" to one of three large cooking pots, labeled "Plot," "Characters," and "Setting." Invite groups to fill a soup bowl with one setting slip, one plot slip, and one

character slip. Then challenge students to "dish up" an original skit or story based on the ingredients in their stew.
—*Sue Lorey, Grove Avenue School, Barrington, IL*

Medals of Honor

Host an awards show for books and present the winner with a class-made trophy! Have students conceive a name and design a book award for your class. After they nominate and vote on their favorites, students can hold their own awards show during which they dress up as authors (or characters from the books) to accept the awards. Tape a photocopy or replica of the award on or inside the cover of each winning book in your classroom library.

Name That Book

Play this game to revisit favorite lines from shared stories. On index cards, record memorable lines from books read during the year. For example, "Without his motorcycle Ralph felt mad at the whole world." [From Beverly Cleary's *The Mouse and the Motorcycle* (HarperTrophy, 1990).] Divide the class into teams. Read the line from an index card and let teams take turns naming the corresponding book. Award one point for the correct title, and another point if the team can name the author.
—*Charlotte Sassman, Alice Carlson Applied Learning Center, Ft. Worth, TX*

Library Comment Cards

Have kids make comment cards to share their responses to classroom library books with next year's readers. Tape or glue a library pocket to the inside cover of each of your books. (Library pockets can be made by folding a small piece of construction paper in half and stapling or taping the edges, leaving an opening at the top.) Label an index card with the book's title and slip it

inside the pocket. When students finish reading a book, encourage them to record comments and sign their name and year. As an alternative, comment cards can be placed in a file box and arranged by book title. Next year's class will find the comments helpful when making their reading selections.
—*Wendy Weiner,*
The Parkview School,
Milwaukee, WI

Book Character T-Shirts

Make T-shirts that celebrate favorite stories. Using fabric crayons, have students draw a picture of a memorable character from one of the books they've read during the school year. Recruit parent volunteers to iron the pictures onto white T-shirts (50/50 T-shirts work best), following the directions on the fabric crayon package. When the shirts are ready, invite parents to an end-of-the-year literary fashion show. As kids show off their literary duds, they can take turns reading book excerpts.
—*Judi Shilling, Dutch Neck School, Princeton Junction, NJ;*
Janet Worthington-Samo, St. Clement School, Johnstown, PA

The Book Chain

Help children make connections among the books they have read this year. Assemble your read alouds in a pile on the floor. Have children form a circle around the books. Then choose one book and read aloud its title. Challenge students to find another book from the pile that has at least one significant element in common with the book you chose. For example, *James and the Giant Peach,* by Roald Dahl (Penguin, 2000), and *Harry Potter and the Sorcerer's Stone,* by J.K. Rowling (Scholastic, 1998), are both set in England. Lay the books side by side to begin the chain. Continue playing the game until all the books are used. —*Natalie Vaughan, Rancho Encinitas Academy, Encinitas, CA*

Bone up on Books (Reproducible)

Have kids keep track of their May reading with our dog-bone bulletin board. Distribute the **Reproducible** on page 92. After children color and cut out their dog dishes, ask them to personalize their dishes by writing their names in large, clear letters. Then display the dog dishes on a bulletin board titled "Get Your Paws on a Good Book." Each time students read a book, have them record the title and author on a paper bone and tape or staple it in their dog dishes. Check out http://home.att.net/~newbooks/dogbooks4.html for great dog titles. —*Stacey Fischer,*
Waverly Park School, East Rockaway, NY

Use with **Bone up on Books**, page 91.

Directions: Color and decorate your dog dish to make it your own! Then write your name across the dish in big letters. Cut out the dog bones and save them to add to your bowl.

WE ARE MOVING ON UP

By Jacqueline Clarke and Deb Wirth

Make the most of those final summery days with your class by celebrating all that your students have accomplished throughout the school year. Here is a collection of fun finishers, wrapping-up ideas, and sweet stepping-up ceremonies.

Butterfly Wings

The metamorphosis of a caterpillar into a butterfly is a perfect parallel to the gains your class has made over the last year. Have students make wings out of cardboard or by stretching stockings over simple wire frames. Then, hold a flying-up ceremony in which the students get their "wings." You can create a classroom chrysalis using a large box or pop-up tent. (The *chrysalis* is the protective covering from which the butterfly emerges.) Open the box or tent on both sides and decorate it with "We're leaving __ grade!" signs. Invite each student to take turns crawling inside the chrysalis and donning his or her wings. When each student emerges, congratulate him or her on a successful transformation and encourage the class to applaud. This special ritual is one they will always remember.

Promotion Pretzels

Send students rolling into the next year by making grade-number-shaped soft pretzels. Use the easy recipe at www.familyfun.com to make the dough. When it is ready, cut it into small pieces and give one to each child. Have students stretch and roll the pieces into long ropes, then shape into the number representing next year's grade. As the pretzels bake, invite the class to talk about favorite moments of the past year and to speculate on what next year will bring. Invite classroom volunteers, office staff, and others for a special thanks.

Graduation Goodies

Send your "graduates" off with a tool kit for the upcoming year. Talk with teachers of the grade ahead about what students will be learning next year and what supplies the students may need. Decorate large manila envelopes with cut-outs of hammers and saws and the child's name. Then fill each kit with inexpensive items such as handwriting paper, a times table, a photocopied map of places kids will study, word lists, a mini-book or dictionary, a summer book list, pencils, and a button or sticker that reads "I'm a ____ grader!" Include a note to kids and parents about the upcoming year.

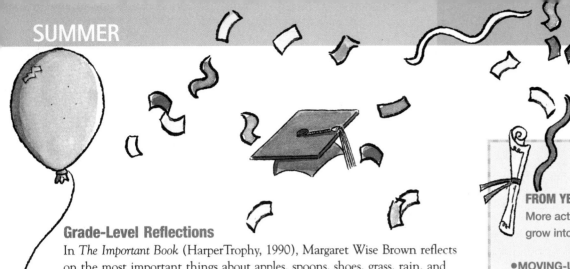

Grade-Level Reflections

In *The Important Book* (HarperTrophy, 1990), Margaret Wise Brown reflects on the most important things about apples, spoons, shoes, grass, rain, and more. In *Another Important Book* (HarperCollins, 1999), she reflects on what is important about being ages one through six. Read aloud these charming books to your students, then encourage them to complete this sentence: "The most important thing I learned this year is…." As a class, put together your own "Important Book" with each child writing one page.

Balloon Toss

At your end-of-year party, give each student a slip of paper and invite him or her to write one goal for the future. Have students slip the notes inside balloons and then inflate them. Later, let kids toss balloons (like graduation caps), keeping one to pop and share its message.

Grown-up Garb

The end of the year is a great time for kids to think about the future—next year and when they grow up! Hold a What-I-Want-To-Be Day and invite students to come dressed in clothing that represents a job that interests them. Have students research their chosen profession and report to the class. Take pictures of the event for kids to take home.

Famous Last Words

Before your students move on, invite them to leave behind some words of wisdom. Give each student a construction paper "brick" on which to record a piece of advice that they think will be helpful to future classes, such as "Remember to feed our fish" and "Don't talk during read-aloud time." Then tape the bricks on a bulletin board to make a wall. Next fall, share these "famous last words" with your new students.

FROM YEAR TO YEAR

More activities to help kids grow into their new grades.

●MOVING-UP DAY

Get together with the teachers in the grade above and host a Moving-Up Day. Children will appreciate the chance to meet the teachers and see their new classrooms. Encourage them to share the exciting activities next year's class will encounter.

●MURAL OF MEMORIES

Take the learning outside! Bring colored chalk and invite your students to create a mural illustrating the many wonderful things your class did, saw, and learned this year. It will be a great "advertisement" for next year's students. Back inside, have your class write about the favorite memories they drew.

●BUDDY LETTERS

Invite your students to write letters to next year's class. Remind them that they are the "experts" on your class and can give great advice. Next year, place a "buddy" letter on each student's desk—it will help to ease first-day anxiety!

●OUR CLASS TIME LINE

Help students create a month-by-month class time line that celebrates the key events from the past year. Invite kids to work in groups to brainstorm important moments of the year and record them on notecards. Then, lay the cards out and have kids work to put them in chronological order.

Meeting the Standards

The standards used by *Instructor* are the K–8 national standards as compiled by McREL (Mid-continent Research for Education and Learning). To learn more, go to www.mcrel.com.

LIFE SKILLS

ARTICLE	PAGE	
Back to School Kit: The First Day	10	Works well with diverse individuals and in diverse situations; Displays friendliness with others; Displays empathy with others; Engages in active listening; Demonstrates respect for others in a group
Welcoming Second-Language Learners	15	Applies basic trouble-shooting and problem-solving techniques; Identifies the similarities and differences between persons, places, things, and events using concrete criteria; Seeks information nondefensively
We Are Moving on Up	93	Celebrates accomplishments; Passes on authority when appropriate; Contributes to the development of a supportive climate in groups; Displays a sense of personal direction and purpose

MATHEMATICS

ARTICLE	PAGE	
Multiplication Mysteries	25	Uses whole number models (e.g., manipulative materials) to represent problems; Understands that mathematical ideas can be represented concretely, graphically, and symbolically; Multiplies whole numbers
Mayflower Math	35	Solves real-world problems involving addition and subtraction of whole numbers; Understands and applies basic and advanced properties of the concepts of measurement; Understands the concept of time
Storybook 100 Days	46	Understands that numerals are symbols used to represent quantities or attributes of real-world objects; Counts whole numbers; Understands symbolic and pictorial representations of numbers (e.g., written numerals)
A Field Day for Math	84	Counts whole numbers; Adds and subtracts whole numbers; Multiplies and divides whole numbers; Understands symbolic representations of numbers; Uses discussions with others to understand problems

READING AND WRITING

ARTICLE	PAGE	
Make Your Class a Community With Kevin Henkes	12	Knows the main ideas or theme of a story; Knows setting, main characters, main events, sequence, and problems in stories; Relates stories to personal experiences (e.g., events, characters, conflicts, themes)
Not-So-Scary Storybook October	31	Knows setting, main characters, main events, sequence, and problems in stories; Uses personal criteria to select reading material (e.g., personal interest, knowledge of authors and genres, text difficulty, recommendations of others)
What Makes a Sentence?	59	Recognizes parts of speech; Uses complete sentences in written compositions; Uses conventions of spelling, capitalization, and punctuation; Uses adjectives in written compositions (e.g., uses descriptive words)
Happy Birthday, Dr. Seuss!	68	Makes simple inferences regarding the order of events and possible outcomes; Understands the ways in which language is used in literary texts (e.g., personification, alliteration, onomatopoeia, simile, metaphor, imagery, hyperbole, beat, rhythm)
Every Word Counts in Haiku	75	Knows the defining characteristics of a variety of literary forms and genres (e.g., fairy tales, folk tales, poems, fables); Understands specific devices an author uses to accomplish his or her purpose (persuasive techniques, style, language); Uses descriptive language that clarifies and enhances ideas (e.g., sensory details)

SCIENCE

SOCIAL STUDIES